C000140956

Bob Mann

Peter Seadalen

NEWCASTLE UNITED'S

PERFECT 10

Sport Media
A Trinity Mirror Business

ABOUT THE AUTHOR

John Gibson was born a Newcastle United fan in the west end of the city, graduating from standing behind the Leazes goal to the press box. He has reported on Newcastle United for the Evening Chronicle from 1966 when he returned from Fleet Street, first covering the club on a daily basis and then as executive sports editor.

He has travelled extensively not only with United in Europe but for World Cup finals and Olympic Games as far afield as America, Mexico, Australia and Japan.

An author of 17 books, including many on United, Gibson is an award-winning journalist having been named North East Sportswriter of the Year and Regional Sportswriter of the Year nationally on several occasions. He was awarded the prestigious Wilkinson Sword by Sport Newcastle in 2005 for his services to sport in the city. The following year it was won by Alan Shearer upon his retirement.

Gibson's deep love of football saw him decide to experience the game on the other side of the great divide – the boardroom. For a decade he was chairman of Gateshead when they were in the Conference and later when the Tynesiders famously travelled to League club Halifax Town, managed by former Magpie Paul Bracewell, and won 2-0 in the FA Cup.

In the 1980s, Gibson had his first stab at selecting his personal *Newcastle United Greats,* which is always subjective. This latest "Perfect 10" challenge has given him the chance to review his original manuscript and while some things haven't changed, this book will once again spark intrigue amongst the fans while re-igniting the great debate.

Sport Media
A Trinity Mirror Business

Published in Great Britain in 2007 by:
Trinity Mirror Sport Media,
PO Box 48, Old Hall Street,
Liverpool L69 3EB

Executive Editor: KEN ROGERS
Art Editor: RICK COOKE
Editorial Assistant: JAMES CLEARY
Cover Design: GLEN HIND

ISBN 978-1905-26631-9

Printed and finished by Brolink

ACKNOWLEDGEMENTS

My sincere thanks to my Perfect 10 for the immense enjoyment they have given me and thousands like me, and for their co-operation over the years in countless interviews.

Thanks, too, to the Evening Chronicle for the career opportunity, the funding for me to travel the world over, and for the photographs used in this book. They have never realised, bless them, that I would have paid for the privilege of reporting on my beloved United.

Finally may I show my appreciation to Sport Media executive editor Ken Rogers, editorial assistant James Cleary and the rest of the team there for their invaluable help in producing this book.

CONTENTS

Perfect
10

Not considered for the Perfect 10 – No. 9 legend Wor Jackie Milburn (above), and 1952 FA Cup-winning skipper Joe Harvey

INTRODUCTION

Perfect
10

Every soccer club has an honours board where men of great daring do are recorded in large gold letters. They stand out as beacons on a moonless night, signposts down the years of fabulous footballers and special times.

Some are obvious, superstars of such stature that even the cautious do not contest their right to recognition. Others can create great debate, the lifeblood of football fans. Many are the hours spent by the devoted in earnest conversation over a pint of ale discussing the merits of their champion.

For a club like Newcastle United, steeped in glorious history and supported by generation after generation of Geordies in their fifty thousands, the list of contenders is virtually endless. From across the globe wherever those of Geordie descent have rested their weary heads comes opinion, both passionate and well researched.

In attempting to produce the 'Perfect 10' I have taken much time and deliberation. The task has not been easy, even if we have restricted the list to those who have played since the 1960s. Those are the players who most will have seen play first hand.

For me, a boyhood Newcastle fan, the restriction fits snugly into my professional life because it was the 1960s when I returned from Fleet Street to rejoin the *Evening Chronicle* to report on the Magpies.

Of course, names leapt out at me. Two No. 9 legends Malcolm Macdonald and Alan Shearer lead the way as only centre-forwards can in black and white history. One of blistering pace, the other of power and courage. Both scorers of a cascade of goals, both England internationals. One imported, the other one of us already.

How can you also ignore Peter Beardsley, so gifted that United bought him twice. A maker and taker of goals, silk smooth, delicate of touch, with radar vision and ice in his blood. Small of stature but skyscraper high in deeds.

Paul Gascoigne, sadly sold in a suicidal period when our crown jewels were discarded through lack of ambition, demands his inclusion as the finest footballer of his generation while Chris Waddle, jettisoned with Gazza and Beardsley, is in the unique band of those who were gifted by the gods.

Kevin Keegan was not. He was essentially self-made but, my, he did some job. His record with Liverpool, Hamburg and, yes, Newcastle as well as captain of England stands as a tribute to his relentless determination. And as a manager KK added flamboyance and flair to his attributes to propel United into the 'Entertainers' years.

Such was the abundance of riches thrust upon a grateful Tyneside that no less than four of that team are in my top 10, Shearer and Beardsley being joined by Les Ferdinand and David Ginola. There is no better way to illustrate what those wonderful years meant to every Geordie.

Ferdie just pips Andy Cole for recognition, a belief that I think is shared by the bulk of United fans. Cole never quite generated the adulation that Ferdie did despite gorging himself on goals, because he lacked the personality and the charisma of the big man. As for Ginola, well, the man oozed class and cockiness. He was like the old Hollywood superstars who captured everyone's attention, such was their pure style. He was the Cary Grant or the Clark Gable of football.

SuperMac, his goalscoring exploits for United make him a certainty for the Perfect 10

Perhaps I can be forgiven for littering my perfect 10 with players of panache, of skill, visionaries all. Football is part of the entertainment industry, something often forgotten by managers and coaches, and as such we have a right to sit back and want the beauty of the beautiful game to wash over us. If we don't go to the Theatre Royal to be served dull and dour fare, then why should we expect it, never mind accept it, within St. James's Park.

However, there is an art to defending and, at its highest quality, the eye can appreciate what those of resilience are doing. Therefore I include two such men in my list, Bob Moncur and Shay Given. Oh, I know what you're about to say, Moncur is best remembered for scoring a hat-trick in the Inter-Cities Fairs Cup final and, yes, that played a part in my thinking. However, Moncur was our Bobby Moore, a central defender of great strength, a leader of men, powerful and determined.

Shay Given brings us bang up-to-date of course, the one footballer in my 10 still playing now Shearer has retired. Shay is flamboyant in his own right, an acrobatic shot-stopper not bettered in that particular art within the Premier League. A performer who has already topped 400 games for United.

Many more were considered within Newcastle's history dominated by top performers. Because of their huge popularity on the terraces Tony Green, Wyn Davies, Philippe Albert and Jimmy "Jinky Jim" Smith had a shout and had injury allowed him to play more often, no doubt Jonathan Woodgate would have pushed himself into the mix.

Green suffered even more than Woody of course, playing only a handful of games before injury brought about premature retirement. Even in that short space of time, however, the wee man won a permanent place in many hearts with his electrifying burst over short distances and his clever passing. The restriction I was given, of including only players from the 1960s onwards, ruled out many to whom I would still like to pay passing tribute.

Firstly, of course, my dear friend Jackie Milburn. Wor Jackie, good enough to have a statue raised to him in the town centre when no other footballer had ever been so honoured. A wonderful, humble, deadly No. 9.

Fleet of foot and handsomely athletic, he was a winged god. His mum must have been a clairvoyant for she called him John Edward Thompson...JET. And wasn't he just! Jackie was the scorer of unbelievable goals, picture goals, in the days when immortals like Stanley Matthews, Tom Finney and Wilf Mannion shared England's front line with him.

Then there was the man responsible for the start of the No. 9 legend – Hughie Gallacher, the bandy-legged assassin. The transition from silent movies to the talkies had brought with it the glamorous stars and it spilled over into soccer. Gallacher was destined to be the biggest sensation of the lot, as controversial off the field as on it. His place in history was secured in 1927 when he was United's skipper and top scorer as they lifted the championship. Unbelievably, the last time it has happened.

From Milburn's FA Cup victors of the early 1950s came the dazzling Bobby Mitchell, "Rock of Gibraltar" Frank Brennan, the best uncapped centre-forward ever in Len White and skipper Joe Harvey, later a European trophy-winning manager. All were outstanding as was chairman and honorary manager Stan Seymour, wee Hughie's left-winger in the 1920s.

Further back, now buried in the mists of time, there were the likes of Bill McCracken, Jimmy Lawrence and Colin Veitch from the most successful period in Newcastle's history. The Edwardian era from 1903 to 1912 saw United crowned champions on three occasions and five-time FA Cup finalists. The team was laced with internationals but none had a greater impact than the aforesaid trio.

The daddy of them all was McCracken, whose influence was so all-consuming that he changed the laws of the game itself.

Wor Jackie Milburn meets King George VI before the 1951 FA Cup final

He was the master of offside, a defensive genius who was the target of abuse more than any other player before or since. He was often pelted with fruit and eggs, "more fruit than you could get in a greengrocer's shop" he maintained. McCracken's ability to kill a game stone dead led directly to the old offside law being scrapped in 1925 and replaced by the current ruling of two defenders between attacker and goal.

Lawrence, an intellectual joker off the field, was the heart of United's great team spirit of the era. A goalkeeper of considerable renown, he still holds the record for the aggregate league and cup appearances by any Newcastle player: 496, spread from July 1904 until May 1922

Colin Campbell McKechnie Veitch was a man of all parts. School teacher, musician, actor, journalist and, above all else, footballer par excellence. Playwright, producer and composer at Newcastle's People's Theatre, conductor of the Newcastle Clarion Choir and a member of the Operatic Society, he married a well-known actress Greta Burke, and was a close friend of George Bernard Shaw.

The birth of the great United side can be traced to 1903 when Veitch was asked to give a hand in team selection. A player with an effortless touch on the ball, in four of the cup finals he played in four different positions – inside-left, centre-forward, centre-half and right-half.

United are indeed rich in landscape. Here we honour just 10 of those who have served with distinction and to each of them goes our eternal thanks.

John Gibson

1960-1974
Bob Moncur

Ah, the Swinging Sixties. When we were Likely Lads and the mini-skirt transfixed us all. When The Beatles were top of the pops, Twiggy upstaged Jean Shrimpton, England won the World Cup and Newcastle United conquered Europe.

Time lends gloss and romance, expands great deals and enhances wonderful days, but the 1960s did, literally, hold us spellbound.

England have never claimed the World Cup since, nor Newcastle a European trophy. Or any major trophy come to that. This was the last time top honours fell to United, the Inter-Cities Fairs Cup winners of 1969.

At the helm was Bob Moncur, skipper of the Geordies and incredibly a hat-trick hero of the two-legged final. Incredibly because Moncur was United's Bobby Moore, a rugged sweeper. Defender of the faith. The preventer of goals, not the scorer of them.

A Scot hewn out of granite, Moncur had come to Tyneside with a glowing schoolboy reputation and had become an adopted Geordie, something he is to this day. Lacking of pace like Moore, maybe, but with a sound tactical brain, a tackle that snapped like a bear trap and motivational and leadership skills which were inspirational. He was built in the image of his manager Joe Harvey, both as a person and professionally. Together they conquered the very peaks of Europe. Just as

Harvey, a jut-jawed, black-haired defender, had lifted the FA Cup as United skipper in the early Fifties, Moncur was to hoist the Fairs Cup high into the night skies of Budapest in the late Sixties with Harvey proudly looking on.

Moncur was also to skipper United in an FA Cup final at Wembley – his Geordie swansong as it happened – and captain his country playing against England beneath the Twin Towers. A true career in black and white with nothing in grey.

But don't let us get ahead of ourselves. We must not reach the summit of Everest before describing the journey through the foothills and lower ridges. Moncur came amongst us way back in the days when another mighty Scot Jimmy Scoular ruled the United dressing room.

He'd been an outstanding schoolboy footballer playing five times for Scotland Boys at left-back or centre-half. Not unnaturally all the top clubs wanted him...Matt Busby at Manchester United, Stan Cullis of Wolves and Preston North End boss Cliff Britton. The young Moncur had trials at each and every one of them but instead he turned down the great names of football to sign for the last club in the queue: Newcastle United.

"Why did I turn my back on all the glamour at the top of the tree? Because, in a nutshell, Old Trafford and Molineux lacked something that Newcastle United has in abundance: homeliness," Bob told me. "And that's vitally important to a kid about to go into the big wide world on his own for the first time.

"I felt like a little boy lost on my two visits to Old Trafford. The superstars were there all right but the place was cold and impersonal. My dad knew a little about Tyneside – as a laddie he had spent a few holidays at South Shields and used to go to St. James's one week and Roker the next. United's name kept cropping up because their scout Peter Nellies was becoming persistent and dad asked if I'd like to take a look at the place. It would be the last, he said, after a summer of journeying over the Border to a string of English clubs."

Moncur played at half-back in a practise match and instead of returning home to Kirkliston near Edinburgh afterwards, United's boss Charlie Mitten persuaded him to stay until the Saturday.

"What foot do you kick with son?" asked Mitten.

"It's six and two threes," replied the youngster.

"Right, you'll play at inside-left at West Wylam on Saturday."

Moncur's response was to crack four goals and his wanderings were over. On October 22, 1960 Bob became an apprentice professional at St. James's Park.

"This was definitely the club for me. Everyone was so friendly and genuine. They were really interested in you as a person. Whereas before I had a feeling of just being a number, this was different. Alan Thompson, in charge of Newcastle's juniors and team manager Ted Hughes showed an immediate interest in my progress. And to top things off two of my pals from the Scotland Boys side, John Markie and Cliff Ewington, were on the staff. I was put into digs in Whitley Bay with them. Other youngsters like David Craig, fresh over from Ireland, were just as friendly. This was great."

The first Gallowgate milestone was little less than two years away. The Youth Cup provided the vehicle and Moncur the romance, scoring the winning goal against a club which almost signed him – Wolves – and setting a goalscoring pattern which was to be repeated in another much greater cup final seven years later.

United had never won the Youth Cup before 1962 and they've only repeated the feat once since, incidentally. So the two-legged final against Wolves was quite an occasion.

Moncur actually couldn't get his place in United's junior side at half-back and consequently was shoved into the attack to add a little height, weight and robustness to a smallish front-line. With him in the team were other emerging stars like David

Craig and Alan Suddick, a 17-year-old whose impish skills had already adorned United's League side.

A crowd of 14,000 saw United gain a credible 1-1 draw with favourites Wolves at Molineux and 20,000 no less were in St. James's when the trophy was secured with a 1-0 scoreline. Moncur's winner was a powerful header at the near post from Les O'Neill's corner.

Bob was to become one of Britain's great sweepers, a player with such an ability to read the game, to tackle and to intercept by anticipation that he was the bolt on United's defensive door. But early in his St. James's career he was used at inside-forward, as in the Youth Cup final, or as an attacking left-half. It took a senior pro, looking at a youngster battling to find a natural home in the team, to harshly bring the truth to the fore.

Stan Anderson was the king of attacking wing-halves, a player with a Rolls Royce engine in him, and he told Moncur: "Don't be fooled into copying me, Bob. Going forward's not for you. All your strength lies in playing at the back reading the game and blocking the holes. Develop your game on those lines."

To a headstrong youngster that was advice he didn't want to hear – glory and goals lay ahead for the adventurer – but Joe Harvey, now established as the new boss of St. James's, reiterated Anderson's words and Moncur's destiny was shaped.

Mind you, Bob crept into his first-team career rather than bludgeoned the door down. His debut as an 18-year-old at Luton Town in March 1963 saw him sneak in a couple more games before the end of the season; three in 1963-64; 11 as United became Second Division champions of 1964-65 when a magnificent half-back line of Anderson, McGrath and Iley barred young Moncur's way; 19 in Division One in 1965-66 and 23 in 1966-67. As you can see it was a slow, steady progress building towards the glory that lay ahead.

Ask Moncur all these years later to pinpoint his real

breakthrough and he can do it to the very day: September 30, 1967.

"I'd almost gone to Norwich City for £25,000 during the summer and started off the new season out of the team," recalls Bob. "I was eventually called up against Coventry City and then promptly dropped again despite us winning 3-2. I had one of my worst rows ever with the boss over that but my exile lasted a mere one game and I was back in to face Arsenal in September 30.

"We won a superb match 2-1 through a brilliant header by Wyn Davies in the dying minutes. Wyn climbed almost as high as the pylons to head home a corner. Although I didn't realise it I had turned the corner at last. From that day until the end of my Newcastle career I was never dropped again.

"I played every game until the end of the season, helped United to qualify for Europe for the first time in their history, skippered the side when Jim Iley was out and picked up Scottish caps at U23 and full level."

Europe...ah, the memories, the magic moments, the Moncur moments. This was to be HIS season, the one every pro waits for and sometimes never gets. Robert became United's regular captain, leader of a band of players who brought European glory to a city which fell in love with the Fairs Cup. Harvey's heroes were men who wrote themselves forever into the history of the club with guts, commitment and not a little skill.

It was the year of Wyn Davies, a beanpole centre-forward who terrorised the Continent with his prodigious heading power; of Pop Robson, a goalscorer supreme who was extremely unlucky never to play for England; of a little Dane called Ben Arentoft, who ran continuously in the middle of the park; of the two young full-backs called David Craig and Frank Clark; and of Moncur, the rock upon which United relied and eventually a goalscorer who brought home the bacon.

By now I was on the United beat for the Evening Chronicle

and I saw every glorious game on the way to Fairs Cup victory. The atmosphere was electric, the camaraderie first class. I remember sitting in a little bar in Estoril, a seaside resort outside Lisbon, writing my match report with Bob next to me adding quotes to highlight the story whenever I needed them. It was that sort of friendly set-up with everyone mucking in. It was a team effort off and on the park.

Bob missed the opening two-legged Fairs Cup tie against Feyenoord because of a cartilage operation when Geoff Allen, in a fleeting moment of glory before injury cruelly ended his career, carved victory at St. James's Park.

But Moncur was back for Sporting Lisbon and the other victories against Real Zaragoza, Setubul and Glasgow Rangers on the way to the final.

Ujpest Dozsa, who had beaten the mighty Leeds United home and away in the semi-finals, provided the last obstacle. St. James's Park was packed to capacity like a Christmas stocking about to burst at the seams for the first leg in May of 1969. Nearly 60,000 were shoehorned inside and high above the popular side kids, arms outstretched for balance, picked their way along the rooftops risking their very lives to get a better view.

"For 63 minutes Ujpest had kept it tight at the back, slowed it down and played it around in midfield," recalls Moncur. "Possession football was the name of their game and in skipper Janoc Gorocs they had a wily old fox who excelled in such matters. We knew we had to take a decent lead to Budapest, and in an effort to get more penetration up front substitute Alan Foggon was waved onto the track to begin warming up as we won a free-kick just outside the box.

"Normally I stayed at the back but this was different. We just had to get a break. So up I went in an effort to add height and weight to our attack. Tommy Gibb lofted the free-kick to the back of the box as he so often did for big Wyn Davies. Wyn, one of

the few centre-forwards who still liked to use his chest to bring a ball down, breasted it forward and as the tall Ujpest keeper Szentimihalyi came out, hammered the ball against him. I could see the rebound zooming towards me as straight as a dye and I knew I must burst the net. I drew back my left foot and connected as sweet as you like.

"At that precise moment the whole world stood still for me. I had never scored a competitive goal for United's senior side and suddenly there I was in a European final engulfed by the throaty, almost hysterical roar of 60,000 Geordies."

With Foggon on for little Jackie Sinclair, United poured forward hungry for more success.

"The ground beneath our feet almost trembled with the roar of voices which must have carried for miles on the night air. I don't know what it must have done to the Hungarians but I know what it did for us. It turned us all into giants.

"I thought I'd had my personal moment of triumph but unbelievably I'd scored again only 10 minutes later. Moving forward from left-half with Ujpest backing off, I played a one-two with Ben Arentoft to get within 20 or 25 yards of the goal. Suddenly the ball stood up in front of me after hitting a divot. I was about to shoot when Jim Scott ran across me. I hesitated, thinking he was going to hit it but he shouted to me to have a go and I just let fly. The ball hardly lifted as it flashed right across the box and into the far corner of the net.

"Frank Clark ran over to me as we ran back to the centre circle. 'You lucky devil,' he said, a grin splitting his face. 'That shot must have bounced eight times before it went in.' Actually it did bounce twice but it counted and that was enough for me."

With the crowd on the verge of delirium United scored a third before the final whistle with Scott, known more for his frills than his brawn, scoring a courageous goal, toe-ending the ball over the keeper before tumbling over his prostrate body.

Davies, who took more physical hammerings than a

heavyweight boxer on United's European sojourns, actually fractured his cheekbone in the match – on the back of Moncur's head. Bob, searching for his hat-trick, went into the Ujpest penalty area for another dead-ball kick and when the ball was dropped short to the near post Moncur bravely stuck his head in. Davies was just a split second behind him and his cheekbone crunched into the back of Bob's head.

But it took more than a few facial injuries to keep out "Wyn the Leap" and he was there for the second leg behind the Iron Curtain.

By now United's season had extended well into June – the 11th to be exact – before they walked out at the Nep Stadium to complete operations. The welcome on the field of play was scorching – by half-time Ujpest were two-up and only the slight figure of Willie McFaul had kept it respectable. United's lead had been whittled down to 3-2 and a slaughter appeared to be waiting to happen.

Instead, Harvey became Winston Churchill and a stirring half-time speech sent his troops back into battle with fire in their bellies. Ujpest cocky, perhaps even arrogant, were hit hard where it hurts.

"A corner on the left saw Szentimihalyi punch out under pressure. Sinclair picked up the loose ball to return it inside the area where I was still lurking after going up for the flag kick. The ball was actually curling away from me as I swung round but I still connected with my left. From the moment my foot touched the ball, I knew I had scored.

"It felt so good – like hitting a perfect iron on the golf course. The full-back standing on the line desperately tried to get a hand to the speeding ball, but he had no real chance. It was the best-executed goal of my three, but to get three with my left foot wasn't bad for a right-footed player!"

Ujpest's wall of invincibility had been breached. They were dead and United went on to score further goals through

Arentoft and substitute Foggon to win 3-2 on the night and 6-2 on aggregate. Moncur, the unlikely hat-trick hero, lifted the Fairs Cup from FIFA president Sir Stanley Rous to complete a memorable story.

Bob is a good pal – I later ghosted his autobiography United We Stand – and he brought the Fairs Cup down to my home in Whitley Bay where we cavorted round the back garden with it and had our photographs taken. Carefree days!

Moncur's international career had begun in May 1968, three months after playing against England at Hampden in an U23 international. He made his debut against Holland in Amsterdam and had the satisfaction of helping his country keep a clean sheet in a 0-0 draw. By his sixth international after playing against the 'Auld Enemy' England in front of 134,000 at Hampden, he was captain of his country.

Skippering United and Scotland went hand-in-hand for Bob. When three successive years in Europe came to an end he captained Newcastle to success in the 1973 Anglo-Italian tournament, beating Fiorentina 2-1 in front of 45,000 screaming Italians and the following season kept up his amazing record of Cup-final goals by notching one in the 2-1 Texaco Cup victory over Burnley after extra time, as well as leading United to the FA Cup final at Wembley.

Not unnaturally, the team had changed somewhat since the heady days of the Fairs Cup. If Willie McFaul, David Craig, Frank Clark and Moncur were still around in defence, further upfield there were new faces. Terry Hibbitt was the key midfield provider with, fleetingly Tony Green and then Tommy Cassidy, Terry McDermott and "Jinky" Smith. Up front were the flamboyant Malcolm Macdonald and workmanlike John Tudor.

Ironically, the Wembley final against Liverpool was to be Moncur's last game in a black and white shirt after 14 years with the club.

He was sold to neighbours Sunderland for a knockdown

£30,000 where he became their captain and helped them back into the First Division before embarking on a managerial career which had always looked to lie ahead of him.

At Carlisle United, where he became boss in September of 1977, Moncur signed two future Newcastle stars Peter Beardsley and Neil McDonald as 'nobodies'. Bob was to make his name as a wheeler-dealer in the transfer market but I doubt if he ever had a better signing than Beardsley, who was then an 18-year-old factory labourer rejected by a couple of League clubs and burning with unfulfilled ambition at Wallsend Boys Club.

"Brian Watson was my youth development officer at Brunton Park and he told me about a kid called Beardsley," remembers Moncur. "Peter was training with Newcastle and Brian urged me to act quickly. So we fixed it up for him to play for us in a friendly at Blue Star near Newcastle Airport. I was playing at the back and had a good look as Beardsley got our third goal in a 3-2 victory.

"I took him to the Diamond pub in Ponteland after the game – Peter didn't even drink – and asked him to sign for us. The very next night he put pen to paper in manager Billy Elliott's office at Darlington where Carlisle were playing another friendly. That miss was later to cost my old club £120,000."

For several weeks after signing in 1979 Beardsley lived with Bob and his wife Camille as he was introduced to life in the Football League.

But by the February of the following year Moncur, feeling a change in direction was necessary, left Carlisle despite his great friendship with chairman James Bendall and headed over the Border to Hearts, where he was to spend little over a year in the Scottish League. We always kept in touch – often I could help Bob with 'inside' news on players who could become available – but back in late 1980 I received a call with a difference. Bill McGarry had been sacked at Newcastle and Moncur wanted to know what his chances were of doing a Harvey and coming 'home'.

It was unofficial, of course, and I put the feelers out, but back came the word that while Bob was extremely highly thought of in the St. James's boardroom, their main target was another manager. The message was quickly relayed to Edinburgh and Moncur, ever the opportunist, asked me to help him put together a Press statement stating that he was happy at Tynecastle and had no intention of leaving.

That was the sign of the true professional...find out the score and then beat everyone to the punch. In lots of ways I was sad that Moncur never got to manage the club he loved above all others because he was made for them, but I quickly found out who 'the other manager' was on United's shopping list.

Joe Harvey decided to use our long relationship by asking me to sound out Arthur Cox, who was at Chesterfield, about the vacancy. It was all on the sly of course, but Arthur was keen, United went through the front door and the man who was eventually to bring the likes of Keegan to Tyneside was on his way.

Moncur the traveller switched from Heart of Midlothian in Edinburgh to the south coast of England and Plymouth Argyle in the summer of 1981 for a two-year stay before, sickened by internal politics in the boardroom, he turned his back on football management to head for Tyneside. Here he bought Gateshead Squash Club and threw himself energetically into his new life.

But then Bob had always been a superb all-round sportsman. As a footballer golf was his second love and he twice won the Professional Footballers' Golf Championship. He'd played a bit of bowls as a teenager too, then came squash and yachting, something he'd first dabbled in during his Edinburgh days, developed at Plymouth and brought to full bloom on Tyneside. Moncur became a highly-accomplished yachtsman, completing the Round Britain and Trans-Atlantic races, which is quite something.

Yachting, running a squash club and watching United play every home game meant he had an extremely busy life but as the autumn of 1988 came round another mate of mine, Hartlepool United chairman John Smart, decided to have a second go at prising Bob out of soccer retirement. John had failed once but this time, suddenly, unexpectedly, Moncur said "yes." First on a caretaker basis, then on a two-and-a-half year contract with his Fairs Cup team-mate "Pop" Robson alongside him as his coach.

However, Moncur's long-term future was to lie outside of mainstream football. Nowadays he couples being match commentator for Century Radio at United games home and away with reverting to "Captain Bob" and ferrying select parties of high-flyers around the Caribbean on his yacht. It's certainly a good life for some!

BOB MONCUR - CAREER STATS	
BORN:	Perth
DATE OF BIRTH:	January 19 1945
JOINED UNITED:	October 1960
UNITED LEAGUE APPS:	296
GOALS:	3
INT. CAPS (Scotland):	16
GOALS:	0

1971-1976
Malcolm Macdonald

He had legs so bandy you could drive a horse and cart through them. His front teeth had been lost on the battlefield and he walked with the swagger of a gunslinger in the old Wild West. Malcolm Macdonald – SuperMac to those who worshipped at his feet – was special, a player whose nickname sufficed.

He dominated the early 1970s at St. James's Park as United twice made a Wembley cup final. It was the era of a new No. 9 legend to follow Hughie Gallacher and Jackie Milburn.

Outwardly loud mouthed and brash, SuperMac possessed explosive speed and his left-foot shot on the run was guaranteed to punch holes in a steel plate. Those were the main two weapons in his armoury but to supplement them Macdonald was no slouch with his head, and he possessed bravery in abundance.

The man had the brazen self-confidence to say he would score a hat-trick and then do it. I unashamedly nailed my flag to his mast, as did thousands of other Geordies. SuperMac was my type of player and what's more we became firm friends and still are to this date. I was Malcolm's best man when he married Carol, his third wife who had previously been wed to AC/DC front man Brian Johnson.

To us all the sight of Macdonald in full flight, hair flowing in the wind and arms pumping the air as he bore down on goal, was a spectacle to be treasured.

Typically SuperMac's home debut at St. James's Park was highly dramatic. The might of a wonderful Liverpool side provided the opposition yet they were swept aside by a Macdonald hat-trick before he was carried off five minutes from time after colliding with goalkeeper Ray Clemence going for a fourth. It was 3-2 to United and a new hero was born.

Malcolm's second goal, struck thunderously with his left foot from wide on the left at the Gallowgate End, was in a class of its own and marked down SuperMac as a goalscorer of rare quality. Yet he was only 21 years of age and had never kicked a ball in football's top flight

But if Macdonald could fire the bullets there was still a need to have someone to fashion them and in that season, 1971-72, Joe Harvey signed two of the finest midfield men ever to wear the black and white shirt. Terry Hibbitt formed a telepathic understanding with Macdonald and Tony Green was mesmeric in a fleeting love affair before injury ended his career. In all the wee fella played only 33 First Division games for United, scoring three goals before a knee injury threw him on the scrapheap.

Results rollercoasted in the build-up to United's Wembley FA Cup final appearance of 1974. Two successive matches were typical of the erratic Magpies.

They were sensationally dumped out of the Cup by non-League Hereford United to belly laughs echoing around the country yet a week later went to Manchester United – George Best, Bobby Charlton, Denis Law and all – and won 2-0. They have, incidentally, never repeated that feat since.

Newcastle won the Anglo-Italian Cup in 1973, beating the likes of Roma, Bologna, Como and Torino along the way before going to Florence and cuffing Fiorentina 2-1 in front of 45,000 Italians. And they did it without their leading striker Macdonald, who was away on England duty.

SuperMac's worth was undeniable now – in his first two seasons he had scored 40 goals in 77 Division One games and as United progressed through 1973-74 towards the FA Cup final Macdonald was their match-winner supreme. Newcastle got through every round away from home and Malcolm scored in every round.

The country was in the midst of a miners' strike and a three-day week which was to bring down Edward Heath's Government, and Newcastle's FA Cup performances initially seemed to reflect the mood of uncertainty. They were held at home by both non-League Hendon and Scunthorpe, though both replays were won comfortably enough, but then they struck a rich vein. Their fifth-round performance away to West Bromwich Albion was unquestionably their best of the season with the 3-0 scoreline emphasising the gulf in class.

What followed was pure United, drama as only they could create. Three matches were needed against Nottingham Forest. The first was won 4-3 at St. James's Park after being 3-1 down and reduced to 10 men. Forest complained of a pitch invasion by fans and the whole circus upped tents and headed for Goodison Park for a couple of games. The first replay ended 0-0, the second United squeezed home by the only goal...courtesy of SuperMac, of course.

Two men – Willie McFaul, who saved everything Burnley could muster and Macdonald, who scored two of his finest goals on the hoof, dominated a 2-0 victory over the Clarets at Hillsborough. That day the Newcastle No. 9 proved that he was the master of his profession.

However, what lay ahead on lush green Wembley turf was the dismantling of dreams. Liverpool arrogantly claimed the trophy 3-0 in an encounter historic in that it marked the end of the Bill Shankly era and also the last of United skipper Bob Moncur.

Joe Harvey was also sadly on his way, the most successful manager in United's history. He resigned at the culmination of the following season, 1974-75, and it was Gordon Lee who walked out at the head of operations in the League Cup final of

76.

United's progress went as follows: Southport (home) 6-0, Bristol Rovers (away) 1-1 and (home) 2-0, QPR (away) 3-1 and Notts County (home) 1-0, which set them up for a two legged semi-final against Spurs when they turned a 1-0 deficit at White Hart Lane into glory with a home scoreline of 3-1.

Wembley on this occasion saw a much-changed United team from two years before. Skipper Geoff Nulty had his jaw smashed by the flying fist of Bolton goalkeeper Barry Siddall in a fifth round FA Cup tie at Burnden Park, and Tommy Craig was made captain. Stewart Barrowclough, 13th man in 1974, gained late consolation by taking over Nulty's No. 4 shirt. Mike Mahoney played in goal, Glen Keeley at centre-half, Micky Burns wide and Alan Gowling as partner to SuperMac.

Sadly United lost again but at least played better than in 1974 and fleetingly threatened to overcome Manchester City. The Mags scored too, through Gowling but a spectacular overhead scissors kick by a Geordie of all people, Dennis Tueart, done for them.

Lee ruthlessly ripped apart the Harvey dynasty, selling first Terry Hibbitt the provider and finally – controversially – SuperMac, the executioner. The rolling thunderclouds were gathering and Lee committed the ultimate sin. Having gutted the team, he upped and left for Everton, refusing to see the job through.

There weren't many after-you-Claude Corinthian civilities in evidence when Macdonald was around, and the fans loved his bowl-'em-over type of leadership.

Yet Malcolm Macdonald's origins suggested little enough of what lay ahead. An average full-back at non-League Tonbridge, he was introduced to forward play with Fulham and graduated via Luton Town without ever setting foot in the First Division before Joe Harvey bought him for £180,000 in May 1971.

Manchester United were interested but dithered: could the brash kid with the self-confidence that youth sometimes brings really do it in the top flight? Chelsea were also sniffing but it was United and Harvey who took the plunge. Joe backed his own judgement as he always did and it paid off…though it cost him £30,000 more than he'd expected.

Luton were in financial trouble. Vehicle and General, the insurance company of their chairman Tony Hunt, went bust and the Hatters suddenly needed some quick money. Manager Alec Stock took Macdonald to one side during training and said: "I'm going to have to sell you. You're our biggest asset and we're going to have to cash in."

Luton were playing Cardiff the next day and had to win by two clear goals to get into next season's Watney Cup, a competition for the League's highest scorers.

"Joe Harvey of Newcastle is interested and he'll be in the stand," Stock told his centre-forward. "It's up to you now, you've got to do the business." Luton won 3-0 and Malcolm – surprise surprise – scored the lot.

Macdonald was told to report to Kenilworth Road the next morning and, after a wait of two hours during which time "every nerve in my body was tingling", a hot and bothered Stock arrived to say: "I've done the deal. This is the fee, this is what you'll get, and Joe Harvey is waiting for you in the Great Northern Hotel in London." While Malcolm had been sitting nervously in the club offices Stock had driven down the M1, completed negotiations and sped back again.

Luton's chief scout Harry Haslam, who had nurtured Macdonald since his Tonbridge days, drove him to that historic meeting outside King's Cross station. As Malcolm walked through the door Harvey stepped forward.

"So you're the little bugger who's just cost me another £30,000," he said. "Sign this and sign it bloody quickly before the price goes up again."

It transpired that Stock had agreed a fee of £150,000 but overnight the price increased by £10,000 a goal! It was a shrewd piece of business by Stock but an even shrewder one by Harvey, as Macdonald became the jewel in his crown.

"It was the start of a good relationship I had with Joe," said Malcolm. "I respected him and he believed in me. We were a good team."

SuperMac was never a shrinking violet, and even though he was leaving the relative obscurity of Luton for soccer-mad Tyneside and the big time, he did it with the swagger of a champion instead of the apprehension of someone stepping into the unknown. He hired a sparkling new limo and persuaded a friend, complete with peaked cap, to chauffeur him to St. James's Park. When he stepped out with fans and Press men milling around, Mac got his first taste of Geordie humour.

"Hells bells," said a voice in the crowd. "He must be the only player to arrive in his signing-on fee!" At that moment the bond of friendship between Geordie and player was sealed forever.

SuperMac's start wasn't particularly impressive. A 2-0 defeat to Crystal Palace was followed by a 0-0 draw with Spurs at White Hart Lane. No goals from the new boy, nor any fireworks. But wait, just wait...

Liverpool marked the home debut of Macdonald in front of his new fans. They were a great side as they always seem to have been. Their line-up read like a who's who of football:

Clemence; Lawler, Lindsay; Smith, Lloyd, Hughes; Keegan, Thompson, Heighway, Toshack, Callaghan.

United went into battle thus:

McFaul; Craig, Clark; Gibb, Burton, Moncur; Dyson, Tudor, Macdonald, Young, Hibbitt.

"I desperately wanted to score but what transpired that afternoon was beyond my wildest dreams," recalled Malcolm. "My first goal was a penalty to equalise at 1-1 after David Young had been brought down and then, just before half-time, I turned quickly to shoot across Ray Clemence into the top corner to give us the lead. That remained one of the best goals I ever scored and as the ball went in, my old Luton saying flashed through my mind: 'Get it, turn and shoot.' I'd based all my goalscoring on that.

"My striking partner John Tudor slipped me through the Liverpool defence for my hat-trick and from that moment the Geordie fans adopted me as SuperMac. For the rest of the game they sang: 'SuperMac, superstar, how many goals have you scored so far?' The newspapers the next day were full of my new nickname and, after just two years as a striker, I was an idol."

United beat Liverpool 3-2 but the full story isn't quite told. With just five minutes remaining, Macdonald was in full flight looking for his fourth goal when the advancing Clemence caught him full in the face with his left boot. He was carried off unconscious to a rousing reception. Exit the gladiator. Could it have been stage-managed better?

SuperMac simply didn't know how to stop scoring goals. In his first season he notched 30 in 52 league and cup games (23 in 42 appearances in his first season in Division One); in 1972-73 it was 24 in 48 first-team matches; in 1973-74, 28 in 45 outings and in 1974-75, 32 goals in 58 starts. That was his last season under his greatest ally, Joe Harvey, and even though new boss Gordon Lee made a habit of downgrading SuperMac, preferring the much more pedestrian Alan Gowling, he still managed 24 goals from 56 games in 1975-76.

During that time SuperMac made two Wembley appearances in the 1974 FA Cup final against Liverpool and the 1976 League Cup final against Manchester City as well as helping United win the Texaco Cup twice and the Anglo-Italian Trophy, though he couldn't play in the final in Florence after scoring a hat-trick in the semis because he was on England duty.

SuperMac and I became firm friends. He was my type of player and my type of person. We knocked around together enjoying many a jar and a good laugh. Life was for living and we did it with a certain abandonment.

Once we employed Malcolm and another old mate of mine, Rodney Bewes, he of *The Likely Lads* fame, to shoot a couple of TV adverts for the *Chronicle*. The shooting was to take place on the Sunday morning in London after United had played at Ipswich on the Saturday. Naturally to us that meant a good night on the town. Rodney, ever the pro, wouldn't join us so Malcolm and I did as much as possible to make up for the disappointment!

Come the next morning we were like two drowned rats while the nauseatingly healthy Bewes was jumping around bright and breezy. To make matters worse the director decided to film the news ads featuring Bewes first and we sat around from 10am until 4pm, at which time Malcolm and I were called for the soccer ad. No one could find us…until the floor manager walked behind a piece of scenery and discovered his two potential TV stars stretched out fast asleep and snoring like babies.

He must have thought we were completely nerveless for rookies, but I can assure you there's only one thing more powerful than nerves, and that's the oncoming of sleep. I don't know if it was the fear of failure or sheer exhaustion returning by the second, but we made our way north happily snoozing on the train. What's more, the ads were part of one of the most successful TV campaigns ever run by 'the Chron'.

While SuperMac was essentially the funster, there was a serious side to him as well. A side I saw – and appreciated – more than once. I used to ghost Malcolm's column in the *Evening Chronicle* every Monday, and just before one season opened we arranged to meet at the Swallow Hotel in the centre of town on the Saturday lunchtime after training. I'd just lost my son Nicky at 11 weeks old and was already sitting in the restaurant. We had our meal, did the column and settled down to enjoy our coffee and cigars. I thought the wine waiter was a bit attentive and the bottle never seemed to empty. He'd been primed by Malcolm to slide another into the ice bucket without a fuss whenever necessary as we talked and talked about anything and everything. Mal knew I needed to relax from the pressures of a week living in Shotley Bridge Hospital with Nicky and like a good pal, he was ready to help without making a fuss.

That lunch went on until 10 o'clock at night before I ordered a taxi and went off home. Malcolm, God bless him, had given up his whole day. You don't forget things like that.

The column, incidentally, was dynamic. Footballers' ghosted columns can easily be nondescript with them unwilling to go out on a limb: you know the sort of thing – 'we played well last Saturday but didn't have any luck' – but being SuperMac he was never afraid to speak his mind in public. Everyone came in for a slagging if he thought it was justified – the League, the Football Association, the lot. I remember one day after Gordon Lee had arrived, the back-page lead carried the headline: 'Lee gags his players', and above it was Macdonald's column as frank and fearless as ever!

SuperMac scored a basketful of spectacular goals in a black and white shirt but the abiding memory for me was on the run to the FA Cup final in 1974. He took some stick nationally for not scoring in the final against Liverpool but, to be honest, United never got over the halfway line that day. Folk seemed to quickly forget that it was Macdonald who had been mainly responsible for Newcastle getting there in the first place.

He scored in every round away from home – at Watford against Hendon, at Scunthorpe, West Bromwich Albion, and Nottingham Forest at Goodison, before topping it all off with two of the most clinical goals of his career to defeat Burnley 2-0 in the semi-final at Hillsborough.

Just to underline that the height of his career was spent on Tyneside, Macdonald gained all his 14 England caps (and his four U23 caps for that matter) while with United. He never really saw himself as an international striker where subtly and a deft touch was required, but more of an old-fashioned leader of the line at club level. That's as maybe but, apart from scoring against world champions West Germany, SuperMac had one great moment in the white shirt of his country – and I was privileged to be there to see it.

England were playing Cyprus at Wembley in 1975 and just before the kick-off Brian Glanville of the *Sunday Times* was at great pains to point out to me why SuperMac was never a true international. Well, the game got under way and Malcolm scored one, two, three, four, FIVE goals to equal the individual scoring record for England. He knocked in every single solitary England goal that night, and if a slow smile became wider and wider with every strike adding to Glanville's discomfort, then I couldn't help it. SuperMac had the last laugh as usual.

What Malcolm didn't realise at the time was that his Newcastle honeymoon was about to end. Joe Harvey quit as manager, and in his place United appointed a brash young manager, Gordon Lee, who hated the star system.

This is how SuperMac later described his introduction to Lee in his autobiography:

'Gordon Lee didn't like me even before he came to Newcastle. I was in South Africa when he was appointed manager in the summer of 1975. I'd been doing a weekly column for the *Evening Chronicle* and John Gibson, a good friend of mine, telephoned me with the news.

"The new manager's been appointed," he said. "Who do you think?"

"Cloughie," I said.

"No."

"Jack Charlton."

"No."

"Lawrie McMenemy."

"No."

"Don't tell me they've given it to Bob Stokoe," I said.

"No."

"Christ," I said. "I'm running short of ideas. Go on, I give in."

"Gordon Lee."

"Gordon who?" I said. I'd never heard of him. John went on to explain that Lee had steered Blackburn to promotion from the Third Division and that he was a strict disciplinarian. "He was appointed yesterday", John added, "and this morning there's a piece in all the daily newspapers in which he's slagged you off for appearing in a beer advert."

'There was more to come. Apparently Lee had said: "I will have no stars in my team," and when the Press lads asked who he was referring to he replied: "You know who it is." Eventually someone asked: "Are you referring to Malcolm Macdonald?" and Lee said: "If that's what you think, well yes." Our relationship just went from bad to worse.'

Lee loved his thinking footballers, men like Alan Gowling, Geoff Nulty, Micky Burns and Graham Oates who used to sit doing the *Daily Telegraph* crossword. He hated 'Jack the Lads' such as SuperMac. "My inherited boozers," he once called them.

Gowling, an ambling, ungainly striker, was a favourite and Lee often would boost him at the expense of SuperMac. One day at Stoke, Lee held an after-match Press conference and announced: "I've the best centre-forward in the country here. He should be playing for England in every match."

The national newspapermen thought he was referring to Macdonald until he added: "And didn't he score a good goal today?" Mac hadn't been on the mark and Gowling had. It caused a few open mouths, I can tell you.

By the end of season 1975-76 after SuperMac had played at Wembley in the League Cup final, the break was complete. Lee and Macdonald were poles apart and United's greatest hero was sold off to Arsenal for £333,333. Mac departed in the same style he arrived – this time by a private chartered plane – but as always he had the last word.

United were going well the next season and were lying third top when they went to Highbury at the beginning of December. They were cut down 5-3 in a spectacular game on an icy surface and SuperMac scored three of the Arsenal goals. And in the return at the end of April Macdonald scored again at St. James's Park as Arsenal completed the double, 2-0.

However, Malcolm's career back home in London was blighted by knee injuries which finally ended his playing career at the young age of 29. He played in the 1978 FA Cup final when Arsenal lost 1-0 to Ipswich but could hardly run and had a cartilage removed two days after Wembley. When they went back the following year – and won 3-2 against Manchester United – Mac was recovering from a second op on a knee.

He finally bowed to the inevitable on August 3, 1979 and was quickly appointed commercial manager at one of his old clubs Fulham. A year later he was their manager after Bobby Campbell was sacked and a new, exciting career seemed to open before him as he expertly piloted the Cottagers from near the bottom of the Third Division to within a point of the First.

Macdonald had some great young players. He signed Ray Houghton from West Ham on a free transfer – the same player who went on to fame with Liverpool and Republic of Ireland. He also brought through Dean Coney, Gordon Davies and Paul Parker, later to get into the England squad as a QPR defender.

But tragedy lay ahead. Malcolm resigned as Fulham's manager for personal reasons – he had fallen in love with a girl called Nicky Thompson, and soccer's directors couldn't live with the fact that he left home and five daughters for her. He was shunned by the game and went off to Worthing to run a pub appropriately called the Far Post. It was a difficult time – I knew and liked his first wife Julie, and as a friend who stood by him I was invited to his wedding when he and Nicky tied the knot.

Macdonald dabbled in football through newspaper columns and an agency which led directly to United's historic signing of Brazilian international Mirandinha before – respectable again – he was appointed manager of Huddersfield. That was to be a bittersweet experience and sadly short. He inherited a bad team, felt he couldn't turn things round under the financial restrictions imposed on him and resigned within months.

Having managed pubs and spent a period of time in the beautiful Italian city of Milan, SuperMac returned to England and briefly took up residence in my house while considering his future. I urged that it was here, where his legend lived, and not back home in London where celebrities are at the turn of every counter and mean so much less.

Malcolm took my advice and today is still very much in the public eye with his radio show *The Three Legends* nightly on Century FM in the North East. A regular at St. James's Park on match days, he still shoots unerringly but now from the lip, not the hip.

MALCOLM MACDONALD - CAREER STATS

BORN:	Fulham
DATE OF BIRTH:	January 7 1950
JOINED UNITED:	May 1971
UNITED LEAGUE APPS:	187
GOALS:	95
INT. CAPS (England):	14
GOALS:	6

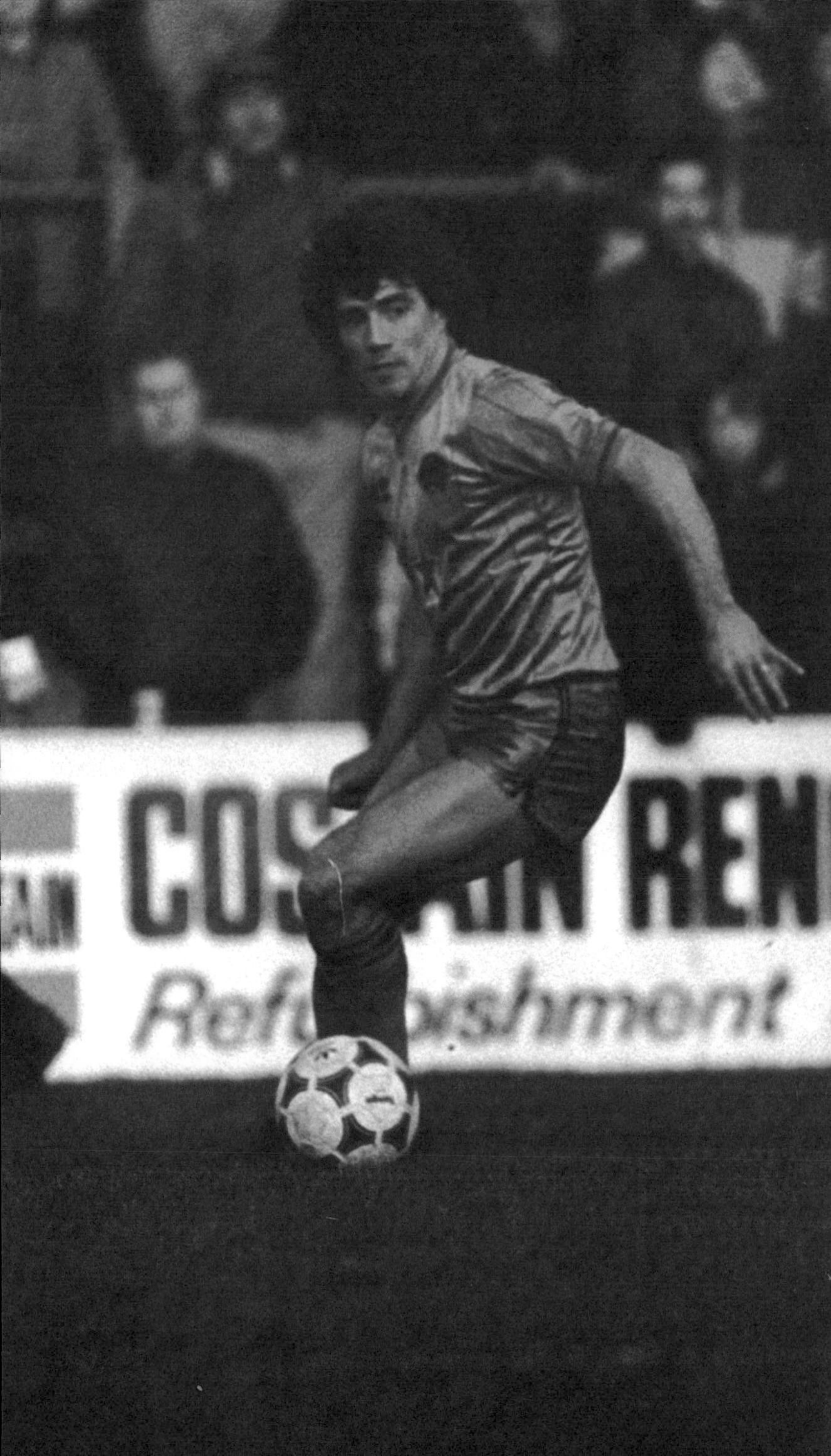
COS AIN REN

1982-1984

Kevin Keegan

At their lowest ebb Newcastle United produced a signing that was electrifying, so mind boggling, that it would rock not only Tyneside but have reverberations as far afield as this great game is played.

Picture, if you will the scene at the time, the beginning of the 1980s. United, once revered but now lost in the mediocrity of Division Two's hinterlands, were going nowhere. The bank manager frowned, the fans lived on memories and the rest of the country took little notice.

Kevin Keegan, on the other hand was a world superstar...twice he was named European Footballer of the Year, current England captain, European Cup winner with Liverpool and Footballer of the Year in both England and West Germany. At a time when true personalities were thin on the ground, this little man with boundless energy and impeccable pedigree was a veritable Hercules.

The thought of such a duo, Kevin Keegan and Newcastle United, coming together was nothing short of a joke. A joke, that is, to everyone bar manager Arthur Cox. He believed that the passion and pride of the Geordies would rise again to dominate soccer if they were given a hero to worship. That hero, he believed, could well be Keegan.

The England skipper was domiciled on the south coast at Southampton where football was more genteel and the fans more reserved. He was said to be unhappy and at a series of hush-hush meetings United plotted their strategy. Chairman Stan Seymour Junior was an enthusiastic supporter of Cox and the obvious problem over money was soon overcome. Keegan had fixed his transfer fee at £100,000 and sponsors *Newcastle Breweries* were consulted on a package deal to put before the player.

In the meantime Newcastle's interest in Keegan had hit the newspapers. He was also being linked with Ron Atkinson's Manchester United, and Tyneside's reaction was a loud belly laugh. There was no way in their eyes that the England skipper was going to come here instead of Old Trafford. It was merely another publicity stunt.

Within the *Evening Chronicle* we were buzzing with anticipation. We knew the Keegan interest was genuine but United, anxious not to cause waves at a delicate stage of negotiations, wouldn't stand up the story with quotes. We desperately needed a breakthrough. Often on these occasions it comes through old contacts – people a newspaperman knows in the game who are willing to give a tip-off on the back of friendship. And so it was to prove here.

Kevin was already committed to play for Southampton against FC Utrecht in Holland and had to fly out to rejoin his club's pre-season tour. The Saints had been guaranteed a fee of £15,000 for the game – but only if the England captain was in their side.

With the match over, it was decision day and I was sitting hundreds of miles away across the North Sea without a firm break on the biggest news story in quite a while. The front page was cleared in anticipation, but nobody was saying a thing and the clock was ticking away relentlessly. So I attempted to contact Southampton boss Lawrie McMenemy at his hotel. Now that's easier said than done when it comes to overseas phone calls. After much to-ing and fro-ing, the nearest I got to Lawrie was John Mortimore, his No. 2. It seemed the whole world was chasing the Big Man and John was his buffer. He listened sympathetically but explained he couldn't say a word. Those were his instructions. Another idea bites the dust.

I was preparing a speculation piece when the phone rang on my desk 10 minutes before edition time and about an hour after my negative conversation with Mortimore. Damn it, I thought, another interruption.

"Hello."

"John, its Lawrie McMenemy."

"Who?"

"Lawrie. Listen mate, I haven't got much time. Keegan is flying direct to Newcastle on the British Caledonian flight. His plane will arrive at 10 to 12. Be there – Newcastle are planning a Press conference at the Gosforth Park Hotel tonight."

As Lawrie talked he was constantly interrupted by the 'beep, beep, beep' from the coin box quickly followed by the sound of gilders being fed in to keep us connected. He was phoning me from Amsterdam Airport before he and the rest of the Southampton party boarded one plane for the south coast and Keegan another for Tyneside. There was very little time and the nuisance of trying to work foreign coin boxes must have been off-putting, but Lawrie, bless him, knew I was in trouble and pulled me out of a hole. That's friendship – we'd grown up together in footballing terms when I was a club reporter covering non-League Gateshead many, many moons before and he was their fresh-faced young coach, and we'd never lost touch from then.

As a direct result of Lawrie's call I met the plane, carried an all-editions page one story including airport photograph of a chilly Keegan stepping onto Geordie soil and attended the evening Press conference safe in the knowledge that we had been 'on the ball.' The official signing on August 19, 1982 was described by chairman Seymour as "an occasion which will stand out in the club's history." Indeed it was. His old man would have been proud of the sheer audacity of the scoop. Stan Senior dealt greatly in transfers of the ultimate significance in the late forties and early fifties as Newcastle marched on Wembley thrice and brought the FA Cup back to the North East all three times.

Tyneside reacted predictably. By the next morning the queues for season tickets snaked round St. James's car park and out into Gallowgate. Hot dog men took up residence to feed the fans, newspapers poured out thousands of words on Keegan's career and TV cameras vied for the most intimate shots.

Keegan had rarely been associated with failure in a lifetime of living in soccer's Harrods rather than the street corner shop and his debut had predictable showbiz flavour. Fleet Street was deserted as its top scribes took to the road. Not only were 36,000 squeezed shoulder to shoulder inside the ground, but the Press box, perched high above the old stand, was overflowing with the normally cynical men of letters literally sitting on the stairs craning for a better view of the drama about to unfold.

Queens Park Rangers, who were to go up at the end of the season, provided the opposition but on this day they were to be merely the chorus line. Keegan was the star. The shouts of "Kee-gan, Kee-gan" rolled down the terraces to spill over onto the pitch and the little man with the 100 mile an hour engine was not to be denied.

The match wasn't a classic, more a memorable occasion, but the inevitable Keegan winning goal elevated it to a higher plane. Turning quickly and assuredly at inside-right in the second half, Keegan stole forward to drive a low shot past the helpless Rangers keeper and in his delight kept running to be swallowed up by the delirious fans at the Gallowgate End. It couldn't last of course. Keegan was but one man and the team wasn't in his class. It took a second season and the coming of international players to support a charismatic leader before promotion was attained.

Newcastle finished fifth in the debut season of KK but he signed another 12-month contract and Cox pulled off the most audacious transfer move of all in support of his skipper. He sold Imre Varadi, who had scored 42 goals in two seasons, and replaced him with Peter Beardsley, a wee Geordie brought home from Vancouver Whitecaps. An artist had arrived and a front three of Keegan, Beardsley and Chris Waddle was to become the talk of the Second Division. All were easy on the ball and a delight to the eye.

Promotion eventually came behind Chelsea and Sheffield Wednesday with Keegan top scorer on 27 league goals. Of course he notched in his last game for United just like he did in his first, while Beardsley had 20 from only 34 games and Waddle 18.

Keegan had announced on St. Valentine's Day, his 33rd birthday, that he was to retire at the end of the season and he did so amid sheer theatre, hoisted from the centre circle into the skies above St. James's Park after his farewell match against Liverpool.

A little man, heavily muscled with tight curly hair and a pleasing smile, Keegan's image was strictly clean-cut but shrewdly manipulated by a master who knew precisely how to drain every ounce of public acclaim from any given situation. That's not meant as a criticism, merely a statement of fact. Keegan was the ultimate PR man.

His contract with Scottish and Newcastle Breweries underlined his abilities as a manipulator. There was no question of teetotal Keegan being pictured with a pint in his hand, but he didn't see working for a brewery as contradicting his lifestyle. His was community work, meeting customers, presenting prizes and working on a series of Sunday coaching courses with schoolchildren at United's Benwell training ground.

Part of his workload involved a S&N Roadshow to go round their top pubs and clubs, and I was roped in to do the stage work with KK. It was nothing new to me – I'd done talk-ins for years with a host of international celebrities but Keegan was in a class apart. I'd seen adulation at first hand…for Geoff Boycott days after completing his 100th hundred and Australian pace bowler Dennis Lillee on a tour of England at the very height of his career. But Keegan topped the lot.

Week after week he filled the pubs and clubs of Tyneside to bursting point. He was like the Pied Piper: everyone followed. He generated the electric atmosphere of a pop star with my voice inevitably drowned out as a storm of welcome magnified at the very mention of his name. On he would bound, a little man with the angelic smile of the Mona Lisa to captivate every man jack with his wit and patter. The show would last from 8pm until nearly 11 o'clock with only a 20-minute break – and then there would be a marathon autograph session!

Keegan would sit down at the front of the stage and order everyone into an orderly queue before beginning a ritual which would never alter. He wouldn't just sign his name. It was personally inscribed: he would pose happily for a photograph and would chat away for minutes at a time with each and every fan. The time would tick, tick away; committee men would look anxiously at their watches thinking longingly of bed but still Keegan would be at it. Midnight would pass every solitary show we did before everyone satisfied, Kevin would be ready to call it a night.

Keegan's charisma drew people round him like bees round a honey pot. Not only fans but established internationals wanted to play with a man who was one of the game's greats. Terry

McDermott, once such a promising player at Newcastle arrived from Liverpool where he had been a European Cup winner and an England international and David McCreery, very much part of Northern Ireland's fairytale World Cup exploits in Spain, came from America. Fleetingly, we also saw the skills of Keegan's old mate Mick Channon and a Liverpool reserve striker Howard Gayle on loan but overall United weren't ready for promotion. In Keegan's first season they finished fifth in Division Two with their top player scoring 21 league goals in 37 appearances, enough to see him deservedly crowned the North East's Player of the Year at a lavish awards ceremony run by my newspaper and our sponsors *Hennessy Cognac*.

KK loved Arthur Cox. They had a father and son relationship much like the one he had enjoyed at Liverpool with the legendary Bill Shankly. But the little fella was strong-willed. He was bigger than the club if you like, and with time running out on his glittering career, failure was something he wasn't going to accept at this late stage. It was abhorrent to him.

He arrived on a one-year contract and if his stay was to be extended then it was to be because success was just round the corner. His thoughts were revealed in an exclusive interview I did with him in April when he stated bluntly that if Arthur Cox left, he'd go too. He added that he wanted United to buy class players before he would commit himself to a new contract for the following season.

"I'm not holding a gun to their head but I want to see some movement from the club," Keegan told me. "I want to play with a better all-round squad next season so that we can gain more success. It's as much for the benefit of the fans as for myself. They deserve so much after all this time.

"I joined Newcastle because I've always put my faith in people not bricks and mortar, and neither Arthur Cox nor Stan Seymour have let me down. But at this stage of my career I don't want failure."

They were chilling words cutting through the euphoria he had created on the terraces, but they reflected the man himself – outspoken, committed and hungry to be a winner. Cox called him unique, and it was certainly a unique deal that Keegan eventually signed. His new deal had clauses which allowed him to bail out at Christmas for a transfer fee of £75,000. If he went between Christmas and the end of the season, the fee would be £50,000; and at the end of the season he would get a free.

If it was meant as a kick up the backside to those upstairs – a safety net against any growing lack of ambition with Keegan safely signed up – then it worked. Cox was allowed to buy, and before a ball was kicked in anger he signed goalkeeper Martin Thomas permanently and brought in two new full-backs, Malcolm Brown and John Ryan, for a joint outlay of £325,000. But it was an outgoing transfer which rocked Tyneside. Keegan's strike partner Imre Varadi, much against his wishes, was sold to promotion-rivals Sheffield Wednesday. Varadi had scored 42 goals in two seasons and that was enough to ingratiate him with the fans, but not Keegan.

I well remember a do at the Supporters' Club in the couple of days the transfer was on the boil. Varadi was almost in tears at the thought of leaving, and the supporters to a man were behind him. But Cox knew what the fans didn't – Varadi wasn't the perfect foil for Kevin.

Keegan, having played at the very top of his profession, liked to link with someone who had a good first touch and could play quick one-twos to put one of them within striking range. Varadi, on the other hand, was not a touch player and preferred the ball played over the top so that he could use his lightning pace. In those circumstances only one player was going to go.

Maybe that's player power but the outcome was to guarantee United promotion. Peter Beardsley, who possessed

the caress of a velvet glove, was imported from Vancouver Whitecaps and with Chris Waddle having shrugged off the apprehension of playing with a superstar (something which blighted his early days under Keegan), the three of them became a potent force up front. Each was an artist in his own right, two youngsters blossoming at the knee of the golden oldie.

United, having shrugged off the shackles of self-doubt, blossomed in the autumn sunshine of Keegan's career. By the time October came round, six successive league victories put them into a gallop and, with central defender Glenn Roeder from QPR aboard the New Year arrived to a similar harvest. One game was lost in February and none the following month.

Keegan knew what we didn't – that he was about to retire – and he announced it with typical showmanship. On his 33rd birthday, St. Valentine's Day, 1984, slap bang in the middle of United's promotion surge, the headlines blared: 'Keegan Quits Soccer'. He was to call it a day at the end of the season and he wanted the black and white faithful to know that he would never kick a ball for any other club. It worked like a charm: the final bond had been forged. Only promotion, Keegan's farewell present to Tyneside, needed to be achieved.

And it was on Easter Monday that poor Carlisle United were swept aside 5-1 in front of 33,386 with Keegan and Waddle scoring twice and Beardsley knocking in the other goal. In the next home game the gate was bumped up to 35,850 as Derby County were clinically taken apart 4-0 with the same talented trio responsible and two days later a 2-2 draw at Huddersfield clinched promotion.

The finale was against Brighton at St. James's and it was sheer theatre. United were up and their god was saying goodbye. A full house of 36,145 packed the ground to witness the very last football league appearance of one of them. United won 3-1 and KK scored in his last match just as he had in his first for United.

But stars always take a second curtain call and Keegan's old club Liverpool were brought to the park for a nostalgic send-off which saw the great man lifted from the centre circle by helicopter on the final whistle. It was a bigger weepie than ET's Hollywood lift-off in the flying saucer!

Following KK was asking much and really United never truly buzzed again until he returned as manager a decade later to launch an era of fantasy football culminating in Newcastle being Premier League runners-up.

In the meantime they sold off their crown jewels, Geordie boys Peter Beardsley, Chris Waddle and Paul Gascoigne and reaped the reward such heresy deserved. They were relegated.

However Keegan the manager was to be as explosive, as dynamic, as Keegan the player. Out of the game and resting either on his sun lounger in Marbella or on the adjacent golf courses, somehow the Halls persuaded him to return to his old home and stir the Geordie hearts a second time.

He did, too, first saving the club from the humiliation of football in the backwaters of the old Third Division, then going up as swaggering champions and finally finishing second top of the new Premier League.

Along the way Keegan signed players of panache and purpose, exciting players to stir first Tyneside and then a nation. Men like Andy Cole, Les Ferdinand, Peter Beardsley, Rob Lee, John Beresford, David Ginola, Philippe Albert, Tino Asprilla and Alan Shearer. What a galaxy of stars, what entertainers all.

Of course KK lived on the edge of the trigger, frequently threatening to resign and finally doing so a season after United blew a 12-point lead to Manchester United for the Premier League championship.

Kevin never seemed to be quite the same man again. A light

had gone out never to be replaced. He managed Fulham and Manchester City, as well as briefly England, but he was a mighty tub-thumper and never cut out to play the crafty international game of chess where tactical nous was the main ingredient required.

However in two stints on Tyneside Kevin Keegan became a legend, loved and never to be forgotten.

KEVIN KEEGAN - CAREER STATS	
BORN:	Doncaster
DATE OF BIRTH:	February 14 1951
JOINED UNITED:	August 1982
UNITED LEAGUE APPS:	78
GOALS:	48
INT. CAPS (England):	63
GOALS:	21

1980-1985

Chris
Waddle

Ugly ducklings can grow up into graceful swans. Here is living proof if any were ever needed. Waddle was an ungainly footballer in his youth. He ran with shoulders hunched as though carrying a sack of coal on his back. Nay trundled rather than ran. Head down, arms flapping, lackadaisical, he frustrated managers and coaches alike who could see talent without being able to reach deep inside to the rich vein beneath the surface.

But as years added the supreme confidence of an athlete who knows his special capabilities, Waddle became an artist. Put a football in his path and he glided, swaying mesmerisingly to taunt and unbalance his opponent, before effortlessly moving away. One moment he was there, the next...whoosh, he was gone! They knew what he was going to do; it was simply that they couldn't stop him.

Waddle, like the great Wor Jackie, like SuperMac, like his contemporary Beardsley, was not blessed with the education of a Football League club from the day he first discarded his school satchel. Oh sure, clubs had watched the painfully shy, small schoolboy from Heworth Grange. He'd even gone ever so fleetingly to Newcastle United for twice-a-week training as a 13-year-old in 1974, and had a spell with Coventry City where homesickness became chronic but as a 16-year-old he signed on the dole, receiving the princely sum of £10.30. A job as a sausage seasoner relieved Waddle of that particular hell of the dole queue but football was still no more than flirtation rather than a way of life.

My earliest meeting with Chris was, strangely, something he remembered and I didn't! Mind you, there was a good reason for that – it was long before he became a household name when even I was actually more in the public eye than him, at least on Tyneside. Waddle was playing for Clarke Chapman's, and being the local sports editor I annually presented their end-of-season awards, taking along one of the United players to add a bit of sparkle. This particular night I was with John Connolly who possessed the roguish humour which often blesses the Scots, and we duly handed over the trophies to a succession of kids, had photographs taken, and downed a few lagers. It was pleasant but I thought nothing of it particularly. It was merely another night of prize giving like many I endured and still do, as part of my job. It was only years later that Chris pulled me and produced a slightly tattered photograph of the Clarke Chapman's team group with Connolly and me in the back row.

He pointed to a youngster in the front row. It was a very young Chris Waddle, long before he became an England international. I remember a similar incident with Steve Cram, the athlete who later became the Commonwealth, European and World 1,500m champion and often wonder how many more faceless kids who have received a quick handshake and trophy have gone on to greater things.

Waddle was confined to playing on the infamous sloping pitch of Tow Law in the Drybroughs Northern League before United at last introduced him to the full-time game in the summer of 1980. Former England striker Allan Clarke had offered him a trial at Barnsley, which he turned down and Sunderland, the club he had supported as a boy, took him for a short stay only for Ken Knighton and Frank Clark to tell him he was no better than what they already had – a decision which came back to haunt them.

United were in the hinterlands of the Second Division when Waddle arrived, and within a blink of an eyelid manager Bill McGarry was sacked. The man who took over, Arthur Cox, was to coax, cajole and even bully Chris into becoming an international. The learning years were hard inasmuch as whenever there seemed a lull in events Press-wise Cox would always appear to have a go at Waddle. But it was his way of giving a talented youngster a kick up the backside. No ability was to be wasted if Cox had anything to do with it.

Waddle made his Football League debut in that first season against Shrewsbury Town at St. James's Park. It was in midweek, the rain sleeted down all night, and Shrewsbury were typically difficult to play against. A Bobby Shinton goal made it a winning start but while the promise was there it was a competent performance rather than a spectacular one.

Chris was still the introvert rather than the brash kid Paul Gascoigne was from day one. He took the 59 bus to the ground, as he did for quite a while on match days and wore a £15 suit he had picked up in the sales. Often as his career began to unfold Waddle would slip onto the upstairs back seat of the bus and bury himself in The Pink so that he wouldn't be recognised by the fans. He'd listen as the banter went on about the match without ever daring to join in.

That first season Waddle played a total of 17 league and cup games, scoring three goals. It was enough to win himself a two-year contract at £120 a week basic plus £70 appearance money, not a fortune by any means but a welcome step in the right direction especially as he was to play in all 47 matches during the 1981-82 campaign.

Such a run, during which time glimpses of the Waddle of tomorrow began to emerge, brought tangible results. He still had a year of his old contract remaining but Cox, encouraged by the lanky lad with a knack of doing the unexpected, bumped up his wage packet to £415 a week and he was promised a car if he scored 20 goals. The Football League player who couldn't drive and got a bus to the match had been a good story for the nationals but it took Chris no fewer than four tests to get his licence – just in case!

Before the 1982-83 season started United went on a trip to Madeira during which time the coach Tommy Cavanagh, who used to be Tommy Docherty's sidekick at Manchester United, got the players together to announce: "We've signed Keegan." First reaction was one of disbelief even to scoff at such outrageous suggestions. But the team returned to Keegan mania. Cox had brought off the signing of a lifetime and the joyride was about to begin.

For a young local player like Waddle it was all too much. The initial promise was engulfed in the barrage of headlines and national coverage which heralded Keegan's arrival on Tyneside. His form dipped under the weight of new-found pressure and he went out of the team. Transfer speculation took over. A swap deal with Brighton, another with Portsmouth involving Kevin Dillon and a third with Tony Henry of Bolton put a question mark over his future.

Keegan's answer was direct – Waddle wasn't fit enough. "I can understand it," said Cox. "Waddle missed the formative years for a soccer pro between 15 and 19. Consequently he has had too much to catch up with in the professional game. He almost went to pieces at the start of the season when Kevin set Tyneside alight. Waddle just froze in the big-crowd atmosphere."

Waddle's unathletic appearance when he was not on the ball made him look unfit. He wasn't a sleek machine; he looked wrong when others were in possession. But he suffered from more than that. He was still basically shy despite his limited success – I always remember in those days Chris would prefer to stay in the dressing room after a game rather than walk down a crowded corridor and face the inevitable barrage of questions.

Cox's job was to harness the player's talents to his real

potential. Chris had to win not only the battle on the field but in his head as well. To achieve it Cox adopted a mixture of encouragement, discipline, bullying and competition. If the moment was right the boss would have a go. Long after Arthur departed John Anderson, a free transfer signing from Preston who became one of United's most dependable stars, told me: "I hated that man at the time. But now I realise just how much he did for my career." Waddle was to feel much the same way.

Chris got back in the side during October and in his third comeback game against Burnley scored the sort of goal which was to become his trademark. He received the ball wide in their half and ran across the pitch, cut into the centre beating a couple of players, and struck a thunderous 30-yard shot past an unmoving Alan Stevenson into the top corner. Those moments made all the persistence worthwhile.

Like a lot of young players Waddle's form hit peaks and troughs though he was to stay in the team. Keegan's first season ended with Chris playing a respectable 40 league and cup games, scoring seven goals but, much more important, winning the battle within himself.

Confidence was something which he had to acquire the hard way but now, like an overcoat in the first throws of summer, self-doubt was discarded forever. Marriage to Lorna, the arrival of Peter Beardsley and the fact that goals breed belief combined to produce a player on the very top of his form. The swan had replaced the ugly duckling.

In the opening game of what was to become the promotion season Waddle even ended up in goal at Leeds. Anderson had given United the lead when early in the second half Kevin Carr came out for a cross and fell heavily on his elbow. Keegan offered to go in goal and so, unexpectedly, did Waddle. Cox, perhaps afraid that the smallish Keegan could get chipped, agreed that it should be Chris, but when he tried to pull the jersey off Carr he screamed in agony. His arm was broken.

Amazingly Waddle kept a clean sheet and United won 1-0 to begin their points haul. But it wasn't Chris the goal stopper but the goalscorer – and maker – who propelled United towards the First Division.

Keegan, Waddle and Beardsley were a front line which possessed everything…skill, vision, creativity and finishing power. It was First Division quality playing in the Second. How I loved to watch them play, creating intricate patterns and then cutting direct into the heart of the opposition. Each of them was a star in his own right. Waddle's final figures were an ever-present 42 outings for 18 goals which equalled his total over the previous three seasons.

What we didn't foresee, of course, was the disintegration which was to follow. Keegan's impending retirement had been announced but Waddle was to follow a season later, leaving on freedom of contract and Beardsley was to walk out shortly afterwards. Their departures were to anger and sicken the Geordie fans and I don't blame them for one moment.

Cox, who had so much to do with the development of Waddle, left due to a contractual dispute during the summer and the manager who was to follow him, Jack Charlton, was very much a different animal. Cox had gone for imagination and flair whereas Big Jack liked the long ball game…"playing one-twos with God" as he put it. His style wasn't going to suit Waddle or Beardsley who liked the ball played to feet, creating through personal ability.

Charlton's man management was brusque. He was insensitive, not knowing players' names nor bothering himself too much to find them out. Waddle and Beardsley became "big un and little un", Neil McDonald was frequently referred to as Garry McDonald, a centre-forward he had at Middlesbrough; and young keeper Gary Kelly became Chris after the TV personality!

It was all hard to take especially for Waddle and Beardsley, but

the early results papered over the cracks. United got off to a flyer in Division One with three successive wins, but while that was later to be put into perspective, Waddle's standards never slipped.

He was, simply brilliant. My undying memory is of Chris in that third game against Aston Villa. He scored twice and made the other for Beardsley in a 3-0 victory. Roaming up front, he would explode with devastating effect. Villa had absolutely no answer. But then, neither would anyone else with Waddle in that mood. Yet he had gone into the game having received an early morning call from his brother Ray, telling him his dad had suffered a stroke.

A short time later Waddle surpassed even his Villa performance. On QPR's artificial pitch he was inspirational. United, unbelievably, led 4-0 at half-time but even more unbelievably, were pegged back to 5-5 at the end of an exhausting 90 minutes. Chris had scored a hat-trick and made another goal in front of an admiring England boss Bobby Robson, and his international career was assured.

The first step came when Waddle was picked as an over-age player in England's U21 squad against Finland, only four years after leaving Tow Law. The game was at Southampton and within two minutes he had scored, helping his country to win 2-0. Chris was now at the very zenith of his career with United, a player of poise, dash and flair. Yet away from the arena that shy trait still lingered just beneath the surface.

He was now much in demand on Tyneside – a celebrity. Whenever I was approached about talk-ins the name of Waddle kept cropping up. The public wanted to meet their hero. I knew Chris's agent, Alistair Garvie, very well. He'd been United's assistant secretary and had left to open his own business handling Waddle, Paul Gascoigne and a host of cricketers. What about the Waddler doing chat shows? We thought we'd give it a try.

I've often mused that footballers are peculiar animals. They can play in front of 50,000 without turning a hair but put them in front of 300 folk with a microphone in their hand and a lot of them become nervous wrecks. There are exceptions – Keegan, Glenn Roeder, Paul Goddard and Gazza were value for money. But Peter Beardsley, good little player that he was, never appeared comfortable as a Geordie Terry Wogan in the early days!

Chris fell somewhere in the middle. God had given him a special talent but it lay in his feet rather than his patter. His natural reserve would come to the fore in a pub or social club. I recall his hand literally shaking as he held the mike to answer my first question but once he got into his stride, with the punters hanging on his every word, he was okay.

A glimpse into the future came when United played at Spurs towards the end of the year. It was the game which was to change his life.

In the second half Beardsley chipped the ball over and in one devastating move Waddle brought it down in the box, body swerved Paul Miller and struck a shot firmly into the net past an admiring Ray Clemence. At that moment Tottenham boss Peter Shreeves decided he must sign the big Geordie.

Afterwards he enthused: "Some of the things he did were world class. He always frightened me when he had the ball." Bobby Robson, once again in the stand, added: "He makes some tremendous runs and gets behind people – and he scored a hell of a goal. He has a great touch."

United had lost 3-1 but, more importantly, they had lost their biggest star whose contract was being allowed to expire. What followed didn't help things – Big Jack became obsessed with big centre-forwards and brought Tony Cunningham and George Reilly in quick succession.

Rumour had it that Charlton hadn't seen Cunningham play – he'd signed him on the recommendation of chief scout Maurice

Setters – and that when he met him at Newcastle Central Station, he didn't even know he was black! In any case, Jack quickly christened him 'Blackie Milburn' much to the amusement of the players.

While two plodders were used in harness through the middle, the highly gifted Beardsley and Waddle were banished out to the wings to get round the back of defences and bang in crosses. Frankly, it was a waste of precious talent and did nothing to endear the manager to either of his future England internationals.

In fairness to Jack, who could be great company, he was a good organiser of teams and he kept United out of relegation trouble. But his style was to play it long and direct, eliminating players who liked to dwell on the ball, and it wasn't pretty to watch for the fans.

Waddle was to end up with 16 goals, one less than Beardsley with the rest nowhere, but 15 of those 16 strikes had come before either Cunningham or Reilly had arrived. He felt that one of the big strikers should have been played with himself and Peter playing off him but the manager didn't want to know.

In the gathering gloom there was still some light, however. Waddle got his first full England call-up against Northern Ireland in February 1985, though he was confined to the subs' bench but a month later made his debut in the 2-1 victory over the Republic of Ireland at Wembley. John Barnes was out through injury, thus enabling Chris to become the first Newcastle player since Malcolm Macdonald a decade before to turn out in the white of England and the first Geordie from United to be so honoured since the 1950s.

While England beckoned, Waddle and Charlton were growing more apart. The big man ran United in a way few managers had before him – he was the gaffer and he took no interference from the boardroom. That was something the club had needed for a long time but, unfortunately, Charlton didn't use it to full advantage. He bought indifferently, using the club's cash as if it were his own and did exactly the same in contract negotiations with Chris.

Waddle never received the sort of offer which, after Charlton's disappearance, was made to both Beardsley and Gascoigne. Yet because he was the first of the trio out of the door he received more stick on his return to St. James's with Spurs than he ever deserved. I've always found it a source of wonderment that the likes of Beardsley and Paul Goddard could be welcomed back with such an open display of affection while Waddle was forced to run the gauntlet of the boo-boys.

His last season with United ended with official recognition of the part he had played. He was voted the Evening Chronicle – Hennessy Cognac North East Player of the Year and finished runner-up in the national PFA Young Player of the Year. Part of our prize was a weekend's trip to that most romantic of cities, Paris, and off we went with Hennessy representative Phillip Juniper and his wife Kay. I made the trip four times with North East winners Jeff Clarke, Nick Pickering, Waddle and Beardsley and never tired of it once.

Hennessy were the most generous of hosts. We could fly from Newcastle on the Friday afternoon, linking up with Phillip and Kay at Heathrow, have a marvellous dinner at a restaurant on the Champs Elysées on the night, go shopping and sightseeing on the Saturday ending at the spectacular Lido Nightspot, and then do a final tour on the Sunday before flying back home.

With Chris and Lorna we indulged ourselves. We walked the Champs Elysées, climbed the Eiffel Tower, visited Montmartre with its quaint cafes and pavement artists, and took a boat down the Seine. On our particular night at the Lido we even met the Irish lady who formed the famed Bluebell Girls, 75-year-old Margaret Kelly, and Chris actually did a high-kicking routine with her for some publicity shots!

Phillip was football daft and a fervent Spurs supporter, so being with Waddle was a special joy for him. Though Chelsea were also in the frame for Chris, it was obvious that he was going to White Hart Lane, though an independent tribunal actually fixed the fee much later at £590,000, which was a record for United.

At White Hart Lane the talent we had watched blossom reached full fruition. His debut saw him score twice against Watford in a 4-0 victory – surprisingly two headers – and he played in the 1987 FA Cup final against Coventry City, but it was season 1988-89 which saw him, alongside Gazza, reach a consistency which placed him on a new plateau. Operating in a free role up front, Waddle conducted Terry Venables' orchestra with all the aplomb of a master craftsman.

His development off the park saw his horizons broaden beyond his wildest dreams. Why, he even appeared on Top of the Pops with his close mate Glenn Hoddle singing 'Diamond Lights', a record which reached No. 11 in the charts!

England boss Bobby Robson never lost faith in him and even though Barnes' development with Liverpool always played a restrictive role, Waddle represented his country in the 1986 World Cup finals in Mexico and the 1988 European Championship finals in West Germany.

I've become a personal friend of Robson over the years and we've spent many an hour mulling over the merits of certain players. Bobby, a fellow Geordie, has never hesitated to label Waddle world class yet never felt the same enthusiasm when discussing a fans' favourite like Hoddle.

That world-class tag was borne out in the summer of 1989 when Chris became the costliest player in the history of British football with a staggering £4.5m transfer to French champions Marseille. His contract guaranteed him £2m over four years – without any bonuses or endorsements which were certain to come his way. Not bad for a sausage seasoner from Gateshead!

A maverick with the ball at his toes, Waddle become a cult hero in Marseille. His languid dribbling, sheer poetry, saw him win three French Championships and appear in a European Cup final against Red Star Belgrade.

This was him at his zenith. A born romantic, Chris always preferred McEnroe to Borg, Higgins to Davis, Botham to Boycott. He was an entertainer who ought to have won more than 62 England caps though he did perform in his second World Cup finals at Italia '90 when Gazza cried and Waddle is remembered for blazing into oblivion during the semi-final penalty shoot-out against West Germany.

Gazza loved the Waddler and his other Geordie mate Peter Beardsley. "I've always been a great admirer and not just because they are friends and former team-mates but because they both had such natural talent," he insisted. "Beardsley was so clever. He could open up the hardest defence. Waddle was a brilliant person to have in your side. If you wanted a break, to give yourself or the team a little rest and also to annoy the opposition, all you had to do was give the ball to Chris. He'd keep it and hold it for five minutes driving the other side mad."

When Waddle returned to England, it was to spend four years with Sheffield Wednesday, propel them to both domestic cup finals and become a terrace idol but then even in fleeting appearances with the likes of Falkirk, Bradford, Torquay and Sunderland back in his native North East, the fans adored his swaying genius.

Such was Chris' love of playing the game that at 40 he was performing part-time for Worksop in the UniBond League. I remember when I was chairman of Gateshead going to Worksop where he stood on the wing like a statue – apart from 10 glorious minutes when he literally ripped us apart. Afterwards I was furious to hear our left-back talk of his pride at being sold a perfect dummy by Waddle – yet, when I had calmed down, I could understand a non-league player's thrill at playing against a true great.

A fleeting period as manager of Burnley was a disappointment and now Chris is an articulate pundit on BBC Radio Five Live, which shows how he has matured and rounded his personality since those timid early days at St. James's Park.

CHRIS WADDLE - CAREER STATS	
BORN:	Gateshead
DATE OF BIRTH:	December 14 1960
JOINED UNITED:	July 1980
UNITED LEAGUE APPS:	170
GOALS:	46
INT. CAPS (England):	62
GOALS:	6

1983-1987 & 1993-1997

Peter
Beardsley

Twice he came to play for United and every Geordie heart bounded with joy. Peter Beardsley arrived to perform with Kevin Keegan and then play for him. Small in stature but huge on ability, he was the perfect footballer, capable of both making and scoring goals.

Beautifully balanced, Beardsley swayed and sashayed his way past defenders with step-overs long before Cristiano Ronaldo discovered them. A clever player with X-ray vision, the touch of Don Juan, and a range of passing, short and long, to awaken the romance in every soul. Some have hailed him as Newcastle's greatest-ever player and I'm not about to argue with that. Simply, he made dreams come true.

However, incredibly, Beardsley was unwanted as a kid. Rejected not only by the giants but soccer's small fry like Gillingham and Cambridge United. How they must have squirmed as the wee Geordie racked up honours and accolades with a great Liverpool side, becoming the centrepiece of Keegan's fantasy football team so loved by every neutral in the land, and strode the battlefields of Europe and beyond in the white of England.

Gerry Summers, then manager of Third Division Gillingham, told Beardsley bluntly: "We don't think you have what it takes to make it as a pro." And it was worse at Cambridge. He didn't last the week there before on the fourth day John Docherty declared: "You might as well go home now. Our coach Peter Graham has to go up to Doncaster for a funeral and he'll drop you off at the station to get a train to Newcastle." Despairing words for a youngster with a dream in his head but, my, how Messrs Summers and Docherty much have regretted them later!

It was back to the factory floor for Beardsley at Killingworth and his £25 a week job, but the man who had shown faith in him, Wallsend Boys Club soccer leader Peter Kirkley, wouldn't accept defeat. It was Kirkley, later to be with Beardsley at St. James's as youth development officer, who had arranged the trips to Gillingham and Cambridge and he also got Peter down to Burnley, a club which had successfully raided the North East in the past.

The aspiring star, small and on the quiet side, trained with established players such as Leighton James, Martin Dobson, Frank Casper and Ray Hankin but failed to show the required qualities in an evening friendly.

It was now the summer of 1979 and the 18-year-old factory labourer was still nowhere near having his first foot on the ladder. Eventually Newcastle United came in with the offer of a trial, and after three days' training with them he was asked to play for Carlisle United in a friendly at Blue Star. Perhaps after so many failures it wasn't going to excite a youngster used to knock-backs but, in fact, it was to change his life. As I reveal in the chapter on Bob Moncur, the Carlisle manager liked what he saw and signed him on as a pro.

Slow beginnings maybe, but once his foot was on the accelerator Beardsley wasted no time. A hat-trick for Carlisle reserves in his very first game against Wrexham catapulted him into a Football League debut on August 21, 1979 when Blackburn Rovers provided the opposition.

That first season, 1979-80, Peter played 41 league games and was sub for two others, scoring 10 goals and next time round his tally jumped to 15 as the headlines began to write themselves.

While Beardsley was beginning to make an impression at Carlisle, I was involved in a promotion to find the North East's Most Promising Newcomer. It was the brainchild of Peter Talbot, the enterprising manager of the Odeon Cinema in Newcastle. He had a sponsor and the idea was to hold a big sportsman's dinner in the restaurant beneath the cinema with a celebrity handing over the trophy on the night. A shortlist would be drawn up with each star invited on the night and the winner kept a secret until the big moment.

Neat enough…except that I was to be the only judge. That particular year the finalists were Rob Hindmarch, skipper of Sunderland at the age of 19; British amateur ice-skating champion Karen Wood; local golfer David Hawkins and Beardsley. I sat at the table with them knowing who had won and squirmed as it became apparent that Rob fancied his chances, being captain of a top club, and Karen thought she was in with a great shout, having been brought all the way from Wales.

But to me, Beardsley stood out head and shoulders above the rest and I believe I've been proved right since. His 'promise' has been fulfilled more than any other. Ironically he received his prize from Jack Charlton, later to become his manager at Newcastle and a source of conflict.

Peter was well chuffed and I did a big spread saying how much he would love to play for his home club, Newcastle. Nothing sensational in that, you might think, but the next morning the phone rang in the *Chronicle* offices and an irate Bob Stokoe bellowed: "You're bloody well tapping my player."

Now Bob could go well off the deep end and he wellied into me something awful, accusing me of luring his bright young star to St. James's. Evidently Peter got the same treatment for his quotes.

In fact, when Peter left Carlisle it was Bob Stokoe who flogged him out of the country and across the Atlantic to Vancouver Whitecaps in a deal which many, including his old boss Bob Moncur, thought was plain daft as far as the player was concerned. Out of sight out of mind – he'd be lost in the gimmicky world of American soccer never to emerge again.

Beardsley, who had only flown once before to Holland with Wallsend Boys Club, signed a three-year contract with the Whitecaps taking him 6,000 miles away with a stipulation that he would go back to Carlisle in his first American close season.

"I didn't go for the money, I went for the experience", said Beardsley, "and I'm glad I did. Manager Johnny Giles was everything I thought he would be, a great player who knew how to pass on his knowledge to an avid pupil."

In his first season abroad the Whitecaps won 20 of their 30 matches In the North American Soccer League with Peter fitting in like a glove with the likes of former Sunderland goalkeeper Barry Siddall, Welshman Terry Yorath and former Burnley and England winger Dave Thomas.

Second time around Manchester United were over for a four-team tournament and Beardsley took them apart. He scored in just 13 seconds and later hit a stunner – "one of the best of my career" he called it.

Manchester United were beaten 3-1 and manager Ron Atkinson never forgot the little Geordie with the talented feet. By the September of 1982 Peter found himself at Old Trafford in a £250,000 'money back' deal. Atkinson was to assess him over the next six months and if he was in the first team it would cost them another £50,000. If they sent him back to Canada they would get their money back.

It didn't quite turn out as Peter hoped. He was confined to only one first-team outing, against Third Division Bournemouth in the Milk Cup and though Manchester United won 2-0, Beardsley was substituted 10 minutes from time. The trouble

was Atkinson already had two bright young strikers in Norman Whiteside, then only 17 but already a World Cup star with Northern Ireland and Mark Hughes, who cost £2m when Barcelona signed him. So it was back to Vancouver for a final season and a second successive Player of the Year award.

By now Arthur Cox was building a Second Division promotion side around Kevin Keegan at Newcastle. He needed another piece of the jigsaw – someone to play up front with KK. Imre Varadi had been sold, and he'd failed to get George Reilly. His thoughts turned across the Atlantic to Beardsley.

A £120,000 deal was set up with the Whitecaps and having been alerted to the situation, I phoned up my "Most Promising Newcomer" in Vancouver. Would he like to come to Newcastle? Would he!

On the night of September 20, 1983 Beardsley touched down at Newcastle airport on the last leg of his flight from Canada. He was home at last and promotion for United was less than eight months away.

Beardsley was to revere Keegan in the way a son looks up to a father. It was Kevin who christened him Pedro – a name which stuck – and it was Kevin who taught him how to handle stardom.

"He wasn't simply kind and helpful, he was an inspirational figure who really marked my card about the kind of future I might have if I followed his example," said Beardsley. "Kevin had charisma. He was magic to play with, terrific to train with and away from the game he conducted himself with humour, grace and dignity."

Like Peter, the great man had a sweet tooth and when United played Manchester City in a key promotion game a fan handed Keegan a box of toffees on the way in.

"They didn't last long", recalls Beardsley. "As we got changed he ate toffee after toffee. They had all gone before he led us out – hardly the ideal preparation for a big match, you might think.

But as usual he came up with the goods, scoring one of our goals in a great 2-1 victory before almost 42,000 spectators."

The only game Keegan missed in United's promotion season was, ironically, the one which mathematically clinched things at Huddersfield. On the way down Cox asked Beardsley: "How would you like to wear Kevin's No. 7 shirt?" To Peter it was the highest accolade possible and he went on to score in the 2-2 draw which took Newcastle up.

But with Keegan's retirement and Cox's departure came a transformation for Peter. First Division soccer was tempered by the arrival of Jack Charlton, a manager who failed to win the heart of one of his best players.

In a book entitled *Proud to be a Geordie,* Beardsley wrote:

'It didn't take me long to become disenchanted. It quickly became evident that Jack liked the ball kicked long from the back, a ploy which did little for the morale of our midfield operators and hardly endeared him to the front runners. But the lowest ebb of my relationship – if you can call it a relationship – with big Jack came about with two incidents in successive home games in late February and early March.

'We were beating Luton Town by the only goal at home and with just a few seconds left I received the ball. Immediately I began to make tracks towards their defence and when the whistle went for the end of the game I was just happy that we'd picked up three valuable points. But my elation was rudely shattered when Jack Charlton strode onto the pitch, grabbed me by the arm and gave me a right going over for messing about. It was the most embarrassing moment I've had in the game.

'Glenn Roeder stepped between us and told the manager to save his comments for the dressing room. I do recognise the manager's right to make his point to any player and I've certainly never considered myself above criticism. But I will always believe that Jack was wrong to set about me on the pitch.

'A week later he did have the grace to wait until I went down the tunnel before giving me another rollocking. This time we were leading Watford 2-1 with just a few seconds left. When we were awarded a free-kick I took it quickly, chipped the ball into the danger area and George Reilly headed our third.

'I was really pleased with myself – George was also chuffed to score against his old mates – but again that emotion lasted only a few seconds. I had left the pitch – but only just – when Jack steamed in again. Apparently he believed that I should have kicked the ball out towards the corner flag from the free-kick. I felt I just couldn't win – and I wasn't too fussed about winning if we had to resort to such negative tactics.

'Those two incidents sharpened my awareness that Jack and I would never be on the same wavelength.'

When Big Jack quit after being barracked in a pre-season friendly, Beardsley ploughed in:

'I'm no hypocrite and I shed no crocodile tears. I think Jack bottled it – he thought he was above criticism.'

Waddle left during Charlton's short reign and Beardsley admits that if his contract had expired then (it still had a year to run), he would certainly have gone too. The elevation of Willie McFaul to manager prevented that and the following season Peter signed a new two-year deal.

McFaul represented an easing of pressure and Beardsley, progressing anyway despite the trials and tribulations, blossomed into a full England international in Willie's first season. It was to lead him to the Mexico World Cup finals of 1986 even though he was a late-comer to the national set-up. Once he gets going, the little fella with the jutting jaw makes rapid strides.

His England debut was against Egypt in Cairo at the start of the year, the sort of gentle introduction Bobby Robson likes to give his newcomers. He went on as a sub for Gary Lineker 10 minutes into the second half and a month later played the full

90 minutes in Israel alongside Kerry Dixon. The result: 2-1.

March brought the major breakthrough. Russia were the opposition in Tbilisi and, because of injuries, Beardsley lined up as partner to Lineker in what was to become a brilliant twosome. That match, beamed back home on telly, was won for England by a 'Newcastle' goal – Beardsley chased a ball wide on the right towards the corner flag, won it off the Russian defender with the sort of sliding drag-back tackle once the trademark of Jackie Milburn and looking up, crossed perfectly into the path of Chris Waddle for a picture goal.

From then on Beardsley was a regular in the England squad and at the beginning of May was on the plane out of Gatwick bound for Colorado Springs and high-altitude training before the World Cup finals in Mexico. United had finished 11th in the First Division with Peter an ever-present, scoring 19 League goals.

Bobby Robson called him "my little gem" and so he was. After a stuttering start against Portugal and Morocco Beardsley was brought off the bench and into the team and England powered through to the quarter-finals before the *Hand of God*, in the shape of Argentina's Maradona, intervened.

It was a packed summer of high drama for Peter but we still managed to shoehorn into it a weekend in Paris to celebrate him being voted the North East Player of the Year. It was basically the same routine I'd gone through with Waddle 12 months before but it was nonetheless enjoyable. And even in the packed roadside cafes of Monmartre Peter was recognised and asked for his autograph. But there was to be only one more season of Beardsley at Newcastle before he followed Waddle out of the door marked 'exit'.

The parting was long, drawn-out and somewhat painful. It was natural after the Waddle affair that United's fans would be worried and their fears were well founded. Peter was offered the sort of contract Waddle never saw but he steadfastly refused to sign it and in the summer of 1987 he joined Liverpool

for a staggering £1.8m.

Peter had left in search of trophies and he duly got them, a League Championship medal in 1987-88 and 1989-90 as well as both FA Cup winners and runners-up medals and a League Cup final appearance. However, following the departure of Kenny Dalglish and the arrival of Graeme Souness, who had Dean Saunders in tow Beardsley was off, but only across Stanley Park to Everton where the Goodison supporters adored him despite his previous allegiance.

The arrival of Keegan, Beardsley's biggest fan, as manager at Newcastle prompted an emotional return to his roots in the summer of 1993 for a £1.5m fee. The deal concluded with Kevin Keegan pulling a gentle con on his board of directors. Keegan cut Beardo's age and fibbed that deadly rivals Sunderland were also after him in a desperate phone call made from a car park in Wetherby as Peter sat inside the hotel.

Kevin told me, eyes dancing at his coup: "I was haggling with the board on the car phone over Peter's age because he was the wrong side of 30. I knew I could lose him so I thought 'what the heck' and told a fib.

"I said that Sunderland were in for Peter and they would get him if we didn't. 'Sign him,' said Freddy Shepherd, who was taking my call and relaying the news to the rest of the board, so I went into the hotel and did just that."

Sir John Hall admitted: "I knew the quality of Beardsley of course but I was a businessman and my job was to protect Newcastle United. I was worried about paying such a big fee for a player who was over 30 and would have no sell-on value at the end of his contract.

"I was told that Beardsley was 32, but I happened to have a football *Who's Who*. I looked him up and found that he was actually 33. However, I was persuaded to do the deal and I'm glad I was. I was wrong – what Peter did for United was monumental."

The oldie was definitely golden and, surrounded by quality shipped in by the charismatic Keegan, he and Newcastle flourished. Any concern of age was to be rapidly forgotten as Peter produced some of the best football of his career and United made an assault on the top of the Premiership. He continued scoring exquisite goals, the hallmark of his crowd-pleasing style and creating them too. Indeed, Beardsley has oft commented that he is enthralled as much by the creator when watching the game as the finisher.

Partnerships are crucial to success and there have been many down the years at Newcastle, but Beardsley and Andy Cole must rank amongst the very best. Cole possessed whippet pace, had a short back-lift which enabled him to zip off shots and the instinct of a predator. Beardsley was made for him. The wee man could see the traffic at a glance and knew the way around it. Cole quickly got on the same wavelength and the goals flowed in torrents. Beardo was the provider and taker, as always.

"He was a gift from the gods for me," admitted a grateful Cole. "Peter was the best player I ever partnered."

Aided by such support Cole was to smash Newcastle's goalscoring record in his very first season of Premiership football, rifling 41 goals to out-do legends like Hughie Gallagher and George Robledo. Beardsley weighed in with 24 himself, the puppeteer taking time off to do a few tricks of his own, and with such a source of inspiration United roared to third-top of the league.

The beautiful years when we were richly entertained by a galaxy of stars was upon us but while United were to finish runners-up in the Premier League in two successive seasons, the ultimate prize somehow escaped us. It was a period when United ought to have cashed in on their stature and gone on to establish themselves as a permanent force in English football but sadly, they did not. When Keegan quit out-of-the-blue

Newcastle failed to appoint shrewdly, preferring showbiz names to sound ability, and the gentle slide down the mountain was inevitable.

However, Beardsley had served us so well in two spells from 1983 to 1987 and 1993 to 1997. He left us after 322 games, plus four as sub, with 119 goals scored and assists too numerous to record. He also left behind a treasure-trove of memories which for those of us privileged to have looked on will remain forever.

PETER BEARDSLEY - CAREER STATS

BORN:	Newcastle
DATE OF BIRTH:	January 18 1961
JOINED UNITED:	September 1983, July 1993
UNITED LEAGUE APPS:	276
GOALS:	108
INT. CAPS (England):	59
GOALS:	9

1983-1988

Paul Gascoigne

Paul Gascoigne was to become a footballing icon of the 1990s. The boy who was "daft as a brush", yet sparked Gazzamania at the 1990 World Cup Finals which changed his life forever. A Geordie with an impish sense of humour and a heart of pure gold, he was a clown with a tear never far from the corner of his eye.

The greatest English footballing genius of his generation, Gazza was equally tormented by injuries and demons. It was said that *Stella Artois* became his girlfriend as he self-destructed in an orgy of booze, drugs, pain, and the mind-gripping obsessive compulsive disorder.

Maybe all is true, but one thing shines through the confusion. Gazza was a bloody brilliant footballer. The reincarnation of George Best without the stunningly film star looks that turned George into a babe magnet. And he was totally, wonderfully ours. All ours, the local kid who made good, very good, for a long time before burning out and crashing to earth.

I've known Paul throughout his long and colourful journey, from a fresh-faced, cheeky kid receiving a trophy from me at his local social club, through his great years when I visited him at his luxury villa in Rome, on to England, dentist's chairs, broken hearts and futile redemption.

It would be easy to criticise, as so many gleefully have, and I have been embarrassed on occasions but I know the person deep inside, sensitive and hopelessly kind, and that's the Gazza I prefer to see when I close my eyes. Oh, and the swaying player bamboozling the opposition, doing the totally unexpected, and delighting a public who never lost their affection for him.

The trouble was the countless so-called cronies who fed off his celebrity, who were friends in good days and missing in bad. Gazza was taken advantage of by so many in a way noboby could have achieved on the field of play. And I'm not talking about Jimmy Gardner when I say that, who is Paul's constant companion. If "Five Bellies" was guilty of anything it was being totally loyal, always there and never critical. Maybe he wouldn't stop the boozing, or couldn't, but he has always been reliable for Gazza come what may and how many can say that?

Maybe he would merrily partake of the excesses but Five Bellies voluntarily jumped on the wagon, too, at the same time as Gazza and picked up the pieces when his pal was smashed to smithereens. Gascoigne deserves peace of mind now his playing days are confined to history but sadly I think he'll never achieve that. Nature has dealt him a very different hand, a dreadful price to pay for his one-time genius.

Paul's story, of course, began on his native Tyneside in more care-free days and professionally with Newcastle United, his first club and as a Geordie a constant love. Geoff Wilson, who ran the U15 team at Heathfield High School in Gateshead, remembers the young Gascoigne.

"He had a round face, round body and round legs. But I've never seen so much skill in a young player – it was amazing."

Amazing, maybe, but the kid with the broad grin and the broad beam didn't find the path into the Football League terribly easy. Born at Teams, a tough but friendly area on the banks of the Tyne, he played football for Dunston Juniors under the guidance of another early influence, Alf Pringle and represented both Gateshead and Durham Boys without having Football

League clubs exactly falling over themselves to sign him on. Indeed, Ipswich Town, then managed by a certain Bobby Robson (who later handed him his England debut), Middlesbrough and Southampton all rejected him, before Newcastle United took the plunge.

Willie McFaul had seen him play for his school but it was youth development officer Peter Kirkley, who had shown such faith in Peter Beardsley, who was convinced that the lad had a future in the professional game.

"He was small and chubby and a bit of a plodder," recalls Kirkley. "But he had exceptional skill. There was something about him that made you feel good."

Gazza has always been prone to carry a few extra pounds but in his early days with United he was a positive porker. In fact, his craving for junk food led to him almost being booted out of the club before he got started.

"I was hooked on sweet things", admitted Paul. "Mars bars, ice creams, cans of pop, mince pies, the lot. I used to stuff them all down. I would sit in front of the television gorging myself silly. I thought it would be fine because I'd be able to burn off the extra calories. But I became podgy."

Jack Charlton, United's boss at the time, had different ideas. He called Gazza into his office one day and told him bluntly: "Get that extra weight off in a fortnight or you're out on your ear." Gascoigne was scared of the big man with the gruff voice – so scared that he lost half a stone in a week and his career was saved.

He had been an apprentice in the Kevin Keegan glory days at St. James's Park and, like so many kids at the time, revered the former England skipper. He was assigned to look after Keegan's boots and one day Kevin gave him three pairs of boots to break in wearing round the house. Unfortunately Gazza lost one of them on the way home.

"I was on the Metro showing Keegan's boots to some of my

mates. But when I got home I discovered that one was missing. I panicked. I went back to the Metro, looking round all the stations, and I also searched the bus I'd also travelled on. But I couldn't find the boot anywhere. I thought I'd be sacked. I was in a blind panic and chickened out, asking my dad to tell Kevin what had happened. But Kevin was great – he just shrugged and said he hadn't liked the boots anyway."

It was during Charlton's short one-season reign as Newcastle's manager that Gascoigne made his big impression. United won the FA Youth Cup for only the second time in their history, 23 years after Bob Moncur, David Craig and Alan Suddick first achieved such national recognition, and it was Gazza who was the inspirational skipper.

In the two-legged final opponents Watford thought they had achieved the hard part, earning a 0-0 draw at St. James's Park but in the return, despite going one-down, United stormed to a 4-1 victory with Gascoigne and striker Joe Allon scoring two goals apiece.

Paul looks back: "I scored one of my best goals at Vicarage Road playing a couple of one-twos with Tony Hayton and Joe Allon to chip the keeper. It felt good."

In the dressing room afterwards Watford chairman Elton John interrupted the celebrations to offer his own congratulations. Most of the Newcastle squad were a little bit in awe of the pop superstar, but not Gazza. He broke the nervous silence when he piped up from the back: "Give us a song, Elton!" The cheeky chappie was on his way.

Gascoigne had made a couple of First Division appearances under Big Jack as a sub but his full League debut came in Willie McFaul's first match as manager against Southampton at the beginning of the 1985-86 season. Pat Heard was dropped, in went Gazza, and United snatched a draw.

It was a season when Peter Beardsley was the No. 1 star with another fledgling, winger Paul Stephenson, flickering brightly along with precocious Gascoigne, who underlined his budding talent by scoring nine times in 28 appearances. United finished comfortably in a mid-table 11th place though McFaul found it much more difficult in his second season until two men rescued him from the jaws of relegation – £415,000 signing Paul Goddard, and Gascoigne.

By the end of the February United were anchored at the foot of the First Division, having taken only one point from their last nine matches. They appeared to have as much chance of staying up as a snowflake surviving in the Sahara. But then the "G-force" blew away the clouds of despair.

Gascoigne, still tender of years but with talent to spare, emerged from nearly five months out with a bad groin strain to bring an inventive flair into midfield and Goddard, a fine team player and target man, went off on a goal rampage. He scored in seven successive outings – all key goals in tight matches – to guarantee survival, but the unbearable pressure told on both players and the crowd.

In one match the normally placid Goddard actually grabbed Gazza by the throat after he had created an opening out of nothing, jinking his way through a wrong-footed defence but then, having beaten the keeper, he tried to turn it into a wonder goal, allowing the keeper to get back and retrieve the situation.

It was the inexperience of youth coupled with the showmanship of an artist combining to produce his downfall. Gazza, emerging as a clown prince of soccer, couldn't resist the final flourish when an act of simplicity was all that was required. It could have cost United crucial points but, on the other hand, it's the player with the ability and courage to try something different who entertains and often wins matches through his special gift.

On occasions Gascoigne was to infuriate his fellow team-mates and his manager, but with Beardsley on his way to Liverpool at the end of the season he was to take over the mantle of top dog at St. James's.

That, despite being 20 and despite the fact that United in August 1987 paid more than half-a-million pounds to bring Brazil's international centre-forward Mirandinha from South America. Mira was the first Brazilian to play in the Football League in its 100-year history and his totally unexpected arrival was to excite not only Tyneside but the whole of the country. He went off like a bomb, his blistering speed terrorising defenders as he rattled up 11 goals by Christmas but Mira was to fade alarmingly and it was Gascoigne who produced the Brazilian-style first-touch soccer of swaying passes, devastating body swerves and banana free-kicks.

Mira and Gazza – two individuals with high belief in themselves – were to argue like crazy on the field. Each believed the other wouldn't pass him the salt, never mind the ball. It was seen by the crowd, it made the papers, and created quite a talking point.

I knew them both well and as a matter of fact I had them both on stage together at talk-ins more than once at the height of the alleged controversy. Off the park they would laugh at the furore, accusing each other jokingly, one in broad Geordie and the other in broken English. I doubt if anyone in the audience could understand a word. Mira called Gazza "the crazy one", and when Paul said his goldfish looks just like the Brazilian with his mouth open Mira replied: "I've just bought a dog. It's crazy, too. That's why I call it Gazza!"

One night when they were together at Ponteland Social Club Paul ended our session by sitting down at the organ on stage and treating us all to a medley of rock and roll hits. The punters couldn't believe it – they loved the kid with the down-to-earth attitude, saying: "Lets have a sing-song to round off the night."

Paul was totally unpredictable, sometimes infuriating but always fun. I once arranged to pick him up at Jesmond Tennis Club to do a chat show at Ashington. I emphasised the time and the importance of not keeping the audience waiting and Gazza said "aye, not to worry."

When I walked through the gate there was Paul still on court playing a mixed doubles match. He winked, won a couple of points to tie up the match and then ran across with sweat pouring off him. He'd left his suit back home in Dunston and we'd have to nip back for him to get changed.

He drove like someone demented, waving cheerily at everyone on every street corner until we made it to his house. Upstairs he ran about, shouting to his mam for his newly-ironed shirt only to discover that his dad had put it on and gone off to the social club! Eventually he emerged to inform me that we'd have to go round to his girlfriend's – he'd left the jacket of his suit there the night before.

By now I was bordering on hysteria but Gazza was as happy-go-lucky as a punter with the pools up. The drive to Ashington seemed to take an eternity and we were met outside the club by a bunch of officials looking in desperation for a sign of their lost performers.

We went on stage in front of a fidgety audience well over an hour late but Paul soon charmed them with a succession of daft tales about how he booked a sunbed course for black centre-forward Tony Cunningham. It's hard to be angry when you're laughing!

Gazza was exactly the same on the field. At Arsenal he gave England midfielder Steve Williams the run-around for 90 minutes to set up a famous Newcastle victory, and as they trudged off at the end he tugged at an imaginary pocket in his shorts, declaring: "It's all right, you can come out now, Stevie."

Then when Manchester United stuck the tenacious Remi Moses on him at "the Park", Paul looked down at him after another tackle had failed and said: "Remi, you're like dog muck – you're always under everybody's feet."

And when he clashed with 41-year-old Billy Bonds of West

Ham, he asked: "All right, Billy?" Bonds replied: "Its my ankle," to which came the retort: "Oh, good. I thought it might be arthritis."

Chris Waddle, later a team-mate at Spurs, insists: "Some people might think he's taking the Michael but there's no malice in Gazza." However, I know that Glenn Roeder, who protected him and advised him like a father, was always worried that some thug who had been given the run-around by a cocky kid would take his own retribution in the next match and break his leg. The thought never seemed to cross Paul's mind.

While he seemed brash and even loudmouthed, I knew another side of a young Gazza. Not only would he give you his last penny but he was as soft as putty underneath. He could easily be hurt.

At yet another talk-in at the height of his fame with United we were at Morpeth along with Paul Goddard. Gascoigne wowed the packed audience with one-liners and a succession of jokes that had nothing to do with football but would have made local comedians like Spike Rawlings or Bobby Pattinson proud. Then, right at the death, a punter asked a question about money supposedly offered to Paul to stay at Newcastle.

"I'm an out-of-work miner but I spend my dole money to watch you on a Saturday," he said with feeling. "Yet you turn down £2,000 a week to stay at the club."

Gazza answered quickly. I wrapped the show up, and we were off stage. At the reception in the back room Paul went missing and with a queue of fans waiting for autographs I went looking for him. He was locked in a toilet cubicle with tears rolling down his cheeks. The thought of a working-class lad like himself thinking he was too big for his boots destroyed him. I had to wipe away the tears with a piece of toilet paper and help him pull himself together before he could come out to face his admirers.

It was at the same show, incidentally, that Gazza

in-advertently got the Newcastle United talk-ins banned. In response to another question from the floor on his future he had got stuck into what he called the lack of ambition in the boardroom and said that could be the one factor to drive him out. His honestly brought a round of applause but, unknown to us all, a neighbour of the then chairman Stan Seymour, who lived in Morpeth, was in the audience and the word got back to headquarters.

The next thing I heard was that the players had been stopped from appearing, which was a great shame because, in the main, they were fine ambassadors for the club, bridging the gap between the dressing room and the supporters. They weren't inaccessible stars but on the same level as those who paid to watch them.

In his last season as a Magpie, United finished a creditable eighth with a late flurry of results but, as with Waddle and Beardsley before him, all the talk on the terraces was of their top player leaving though he had another year of his contract to go.

Gazza's impishness, his showmanship, was rewarded when he was voted our North East Player of the Year and nationally lifted the PFA's Young Player of the Year award. He was an established member of the England U21 team and it all led to a thirst for medals which could be won on faraway battlefields.

There was no question that Gascoigne wanted to tread the path of Beardsley to Liverpool but the champions, well stocked in midfield, weren't in a rush to take a 21-year-old, however talented. That left Spurs and Manchester United in a two-way battle.

Roeder felt that his prodigy would be best served by staying another two years at United and feared for him in the bright lights of London. But the dye had been cast, Paul had made his stand and it was Tottenham Hotspur who met the asking price, a staggering record £2m for a player yet to win a full England cap.

Potential had never come so dear and Gascoigne, perhaps not surprisingly, was greeted with a welter of bad publicity when he arrived on the doorstep of Fleet Street in the close season of 1988. Here was an arrogant but highly likeable young kid used to being able to go for a pint at his local or Tuxedo nightclub without causing a flicker suddenly thrust into the centre of attention. Standing with a pint in his hand laughing loudly with his Geordie mates, he was so liable to create the wrong impression in tabloids looking for a sensational story. All the fears of Roeder seemed to be coming true.

By sheer coincidence Spurs' first match against Coventry City was postponed because their new stand wasn't safe – and that meant his debut was at Newcastle. He was greeted with a barrage of *Mars* bars thrown onto the pitch, taunted with chants of 'Fat Boy' and substituted with cramp before the end.

But slowly his ability began to come through and the stories changed from off-the-field eye-openers to on-field joy. Gascoigne was hailed for his entertainment value in a time of anonymous, grey players. He blew kisses to opponents, stuck his tongue out at referees and shoved the ball up his jersey to conduct the terrace chants of 'Fat Boy'.

Waddle enthused: "Gazza has always been the same and always will be. He loves entertaining the crowd but it's not an act. He's exactly the same personality in training when he doesn't have an audience. And I can't see it ever being knocked out of him. He really is a one-off in this day and age."

Gascoigne himself saw his role in simple terms. "If I achieve anything in my career it would be nice to put a smile back on the face of soccer. People want to be entertained and excited and if they think I'm a showman that's okay by me.

"If I thought someone looked at a newspaper, saw I was playing in town and came along to watch, that would give me a lot of satisfaction. There isn't a man in this country who doesn't like a laugh and I think football should be fun."

Bobby Robson introduced Gazza to the full England team via substitute appearances during his first season at Spurs and we talked at length about the Geordie boy with the touch of genius when I visited the Football Association headquarters at Lancaster Gate in London.

"He's the most precocious youngster I've ever met in my life," Bobby told me. "He could be exceptional as a player. Gazza is a real *Jack the Lad* but we mustn't take too much of that away from him. All the great players – George Best, Bobby Charlton and Denis Law – had that burning self-belief and so has Gascoigne."

He recalled with relish a typical story about the newcomer in England's squad. Prior to a big international at Wembley Robson took the England players to a snooty golf club in Surrey to play a round and then have dinner. Bobby made a formal speech which was responded to by the club captain. All very sedate and nice.

"Then, for some reason, someone suggested that Gazza should have a few words. He was the youngest member of the international squad, but far from being overawed he got up and told a succession of dirty stories that completely broke the ice and had the whole place in uproar."

Spurs were the making and almost the breaking of Gazza. He developed a wonderful relationship with Terry Venables, an innovative coach and the fans warmed to his sheer impertinence. However, disaster lay ahead, as it has so often.

A wonderful FA Cup run highlighted by a succession of great goals saw Gazza somehow recover from a double hernia operation to play in the semi-final against arch rivals Arsenal and singe the hair of England goalkeeper David Seaman with a breathtaking goal, a 30-yard free-kick.

However, in the final of 1991 against Nottingham Forest, hyped up, Gascoigne scythed down Gary Charles and injured himself terribly in the process. Spurs were out of it and Gazza was out of it, the cruciate ligaments of his right knee destroyed. What a goodbye to White Hart Lane. Lazio was next up. La Dolce Vita. Rome in exchange for £5.5m.

In three seasons Paul played only 47 league and cup matches because of injury yet became a cult hero, scoring in the bitter derby against Roma. I flew out to the Italian capital to stay with Gazza and witnessed the Geordie superstar at first hand, the private man behind the public face.

My newspaper had booked me into a hotel but Paul would have none of it. He moved me into his villa where I lived not only for the duration of my stay but three extra days after being persuaded by him to take in the weekend and Lazio's match against Napoli.

Gazza was obsessed by motorbikes – he had no fewer than nine Harley-Davidsons at one stage. However Lazio, realising they had precious cargo on their hands but one hell-bent on self-destruction, banned him from driving to training on his power machine. So what did our Geordie jester do? Donned a German Second World War helmet, drove through the choking Rome traffic with me and his dad in a vehicle behind him, parked his bike in a garage just around the corner from the training ground, leaped into our car and arrived all sweetness and light.

On the way home Gazza would flick a switch to electronically open the gates to his villa, roar up the long driveway straight through the open patio windows, park his Harley-Davidson on the sheepskin rug, take off his German helmet and plonk himself in an armchair to watch videos of Elvis!

The punters adored him of course because he actually became one of them. Kevin Keegan had been spouting on publicly about how Gazza ought to go to night school to learn to speak Italian, just as Keegan had attended German classes upon joining Hamburg. Well, I was shocked to hear a supposedly thick Geordie chatting to all around him in Italian, especially the kids. He had picked up the language on the hoof and it was well appreciated by the natives.

On the way to the Sunday game we got caught up in a traffic jam in an underpass and Gazza was spotted. From every car an excited babbling fan emerged to kiss Gascoigne on both cheeks and drape him in the blue scarf of Lazio taken from around their own neck.

Rome of course gave way to Glasgow and his last big hurrah. Three good seasons with Rangers saw Paul pick up the only winners medals of his career and perform in the European Champions League for the first time. He stupidly played an imaginary flute in an *Old Firm* derby at Celtic, sparking death threats supposedly from the IRA, and scored a quite delicious goal against Scotland at Wembley during Euro '96. He flicked the ball over a stranded Colin Hendry's head with one foot and volleyed it home past Andy Goram first time with the other – and promptly lay full length on the turf to have imaginary pints poured down his neck by delighted England team-mates in an obvious two-fingered salute to the famous dentist's chair scandal in Hong Kong prior to the tournament.

However, from Glasgow it was a downward slope, gentle at first with Middlesbrough and Everton as his personal problems – drinking and pill popping – kicked in, then hurtling into oblivion at Burnley, Gansu Tianma in China and Boston United in League Two as a player-coach.

Despite this I still witnessed the generous soul beneath the chaos. I was chairman of Gateshead for 11 years and when we hit massive financial problems with our main sponsor pulling out mid-season I unashamedly called on my friends in football to help bail us out. Alan Shearer did a talk-in free of charge at St. James's Park and Gazza, a Gateshead lad, fronted a sporting dinner for nowt. He sold out 750 tickets at 30-odd quid a head in 24 hours, such was his pulling power despite all that was happening around him.

Of course I got 'the treatment.' When my back was turned making an announcement on the mike, Paul would move in. Peppering my steak, spiking my drink and generally causing chaos, all to the amusement of the watching punters. Of course it was childish but it was pure Gazza and, bless him, I didn't mind one little bit. I knew what was going on, just as a dad knows what his kid is up to but still plays the game.

PAUL GASCOIGNE - CAREER STATS

BORN:	Gateshead
DATE OF BIRTH:	May 27 1967
JOINED UNITED:	July 1983
UNITED LEAGUE APPS:	92
GOALS:	21
INT. CAPS (England):	57
GOALS:	10

Bob Moncur (second left) scores the opening goal in the 1969 Inter-Cities Fairs Cup final, first leg against Ujpest Dozsa at St. James's Park

The two captains (Bob and Liverpool's Emlyn Hughes) share a joke with referee Gordon Kew at the coin toss before the 1974 FA Cup final

The 1969 Inter-Cities Fairs Cup is held aloft by Bob outside St. James's Park

Bob celebrates United's FA Cup semi-final defeat of Burnley in 1974

Footballs are on the mind of Magpies star striker Malcolm
Macdonald at this pre-season photocall at St. James's Park

Malcolm Macdonald lashes home one of his two goals past Burnley keeper Alan
Stevenson in the 1974 FA Cup semi-final (top), and celebrates accordingly (above)

Kevin Keegan is closely marked by a Shrewsbury Town defender, 1982

A warm welcome for Keegan at Shrewsbury Town's Gay
Meadow ground, with the autograph hunters out in force

Chris Waddle strikes on the plastic pitch of QPR's Loftus Road stadium

Chris Waddle on the run against Stoke City at the Victoria Ground

Peter Beardsley and Chris Waddle team up against Bryan Robson at Old Trafford

Paul Gascoigne celebrates a goal with team-mate Peter Beardsley

Gazza on the run against Nottingham Forest at the City Ground

Top: Kevin Keegan celebrating Second Division survival with Liam O'Brien, 1992 and (above) the fans pay their tribute to the legend in the wake of his resignation, 1997

David Ginola blasts home his first goal for Newcastle, at Sheffield Wednesday in 1995

Ginola and John Beresford celebrate the Frenchman's wonder strike against Manchester United in the famous 5-0 victory at St. James's, 1996

Manager Kevin Keegan welcomes Les Ferdinand to Newcastle, 1995

Ferdinand heads home the third goal in the 5-0 mauling of Man Utd, December 1996

David Ginola congratulates Les Ferdinand following his goal at Aston Villa, 1995

A deserved member of the Perfect 10 - goalkeeper Shay Given

Goalkeeping heroics from Shay Given to keep out this Charlton effort at The Valley

A familiar salute, as Alan Shearer celebrates one of his two goals in the 2-2 European
Champions League draw against Inter Milan at the San Siro, March 2003

Shearer does it again, this time a late equaliser against Leeds
United at Elland Road in the Premiership opener of 2003-04

Penalty king - One of Shearer's final goals for Newcastle,
from the penalty spot against Tottenham in April 2006

Toon fans show their appreication for a United legend

The final act - Alan and team-mates celebrate his final goal for Newcastle, the second goal in the 4-1 victory at Sunderland (top), and St. James's Park gives thanks (above)

1995-1997

David Ginola

In many ways, David Ginola was the perfect public image of Kevin Keegan's fabulous fantasy football team of the 1990s. If ever a man looked the part he was destined to play it was this elegant, strutting Frenchman. Smoulderingly handsome with long flowing locks, sparkling blue bedroom eyes and an accent distinctly chic, Ginola was a pin-up adored by the women and loved by the men because of the swaggering class he brought to United. He stood for what Keegan worshipped – panache, skill, arrogance, entertainment.

Keegan's parade of champions assembled at St. James's Park to entertain not just the Geordies, but a receptive nation as well that was mightily impressed...Andy Cole, Les Ferdinand, Peter Beardsley, Barry Venison, Warren Barton, Rob Lee, John Beresford, Philippe Albert, Darren Peacock, David Batty, Tino Asprilla and finally, Alan Shearer.

However, none quite captured the physical appearance of a Hollywood superstar to combine with charm, charisma and devastating ability quite like Ginola, even born on the right side of the tracks in the millionaires' playground of St. Tropez and splendidly christened David Desire Marc Ginola.

A player unheard of in many North East homes before he quit French giants Paris St Germain to sign for Newcastle on that momentous day in July of 1995. Yet Ginola's impact was that of an atom bomb. He exploded upon the Premiership and startled even the hardened, seen-it-all-before brigade. Terry McDermott, a man who won the European Cup three times with Liverpool and who was Keegan's right-hand man at the time, was so mesmerised by the Frenchman's performance in his first training session that he rushed over to KK to ask how on earth he had discovered such a diamond.

"Ginola was tailor-made for us," insisted Keegan. "I'd never seen a player like him before. Newcastle supporters want to be entertained. They would rather see a magnificent draw than a 1-0 win ground out through defensive tactics, and David was ideal for the way I like to play."

Freddy Shepherd declared that David and his model wife Coraline "looked like a couple of film stars, and we treated them accordingly. David was a special player and we went the extra mile to get him."

When, upon completing formalities, a proud Sir John Hall escorted David and Coraline into the Strawberry pub outside of St. James's Park on a goodwill visit, the locals almost choked on their Brown Ale. Never had so much beauty been housed in the men's bar of a local!

I met Ginola shortly after his £2.5m transfer was sealed and he lived up to that star billing. He swept into St. James's Park like royalty, ordering a private box and some coffee for our in-depth interview. With his tracksuit trousers rolled up to his knees, he calmly reached into his holdall to produce a packet and he withdrew a long thin-tipped cigarette. "Do you mind if I smoke?" he enquired. Apart from Wor Jackie having a fag in the Wembley dressing room at half-time, smoking was virtually unheard of amongst English footballers, where the culture was pints and plenty of them. But on the continent most players partook, as I had discovered when staying with Paul Gascoigne in Rome and meeting his Lazio team-mates.

Ginola's Parisian lifestyle had been very different to that of the English player. He would play backgammon, dine out with artists and intellectuals in the French capital's myriad of mouth-watering eateries. His close friend was Nino Cerurri, for whom he modelled on the Paris catwalk as a personal favour.

Ginola's day-time job was to partner World Footballer of the Year George Weah. "Many, many managers felt that we were the best two in France," David told me without a flicker of false modesty. "We went well together for four years and we experienced many great successes."

They included helping PSG win the French championship, when Ginola top-scored with 13 goals in 38 matches, two French Cups and the French League Cup as well as reaching the semi-finals of the European Champions Cup. Ginola's Gallic flair had been pitted against the likes of Real Madrid, Juventus and AC Milan; and against top quality players of the calibre of Baggio, Zola, Fonseca, Butragueno, Baresi, Cantona, Vialli, Platt and Waddle.

Yet, Ginola was to tell me he was thrown on soccer's scrapheap at the age of 16. "I had decided to join Nice. I studied during the day and trained with them at night, but then the club told me that I didn't have what it took to be a professional footballer. My world was shattered, my dreams gone." Hardly Nice, was it?

However, a year later Toulon decided to take a chance on the young Ginola who ravenously learned and developed his game. In 1988 he was transferred to Marta Racing Paris, an ill-fated club which would hit financial troubles, but where David tasted his first success playing in the French Cup final.

Ginola's next move took him to Brittany to play for Brest and brought his first French international cap. His final destination on his personal Tour de France was Paris, where he lived elegantly for four years until Keegan and Newcastle came calling.

Maybe Tyneside isn't quite Paris or St. Tropez but Ginola was to take over, become king of the nightclubs and prince of wingers. His impact was immediate and devastating.

I recall clinching a glamour friendly with United for my club Gateshead – I was chairman – before the season opened. It was arranged through my friendship with Sir John Hall, whose campaign to smash open the doors to the boardroom of an inner-looking club I had fronted over three eventful and sometimes bloody years. As a consequence of that closeness Kevin Keegan sent his complete United first team to the International Stadium, which meant new signings Ginola and Les Ferdinand were to play their first games on Tyneside right in my backyard.

We sold out the ground capacity of 11,900 in a blink of an eye, which was sensational, and on the night I made a point of going into our dressing room before the match and warning manager and players that the gate money about to nestle in our bank account would keep us alive for nearly the whole season. As it was down to United's generosity, there was thus to be no kicking of opponents thank you very much! All in the dressing room nodded in agreement.

I had hardly settled proudly into the directors' box to watch my two teams play one another than Mark Hine, who was, shall we say a combative little midfielder, scythed down Ginola. Over went the elegant Frenchman in a shower of flying hair and pained expression. We got the full treatment only foreign players can express...forward rolls for nigh on 100 yards, shin clutched tightly in two hands.

Almost as one every United director and backroom staff member turned round to fix me with a glare which could have halted a herd of bison at 50 paces. I was out of my seat and downstairs like a shot to shout obscenities at our bench. Luckily Ginola surfaced like a wounded stag, flicked back his flowing locks, and deigned to treat us all to the sort of awesome skill we were to treasure in the months ahead.

On the big stage Ginola opened in spectacular style, United's orchestrator-in-chief beautifully balanced and mesmerising. Wearing the No. 10 shirt, he helped United to two three-goal wins over Coventry City at home and Bolton Wanderers away before scoring his first black and white goal at Sheffield Wednesday (2-0). However, it was his next match at St. James's Park which confirmed to me that we were watching genius.

Middlesbrough doubled up defenders on him, like guys on a tandem. The second one ready to hit him if he emerged from the first challenge. It made absolutely no difference. A sway of the hips, feet perfectly still and Ginola was through an impossibly small gap and away. A Les Ferdinand goal, his fourth in four games, and Boro were beaten.

The first season was the epitome of Keegan's reign. United were a joy to watch as Ginola played 34 of the 38 Premiership games and totted up a home record of 17 wins, one draw and only one defeat with 38 goals scored and a mere nine conceded. That defeat, of course, was significantly against champions-elect Manchester United when Eric Cantona scored to complete the double over the Mags who had dominated, particularly in the first half.

If Ginola was a magician on the ball, there was never any help defensively from a swaggering star who viewed tracking back as a job for a hod carrier. I've worked a lot on the talk-in circuit with John Beresford in recent times and I always rib him that before he played directly behind Ginola he was 6ft 3ins – but got ground into the dirt!

"I was often left with two overlapping players bearing down on me while David preened himself on the halfway line waiting until we won the ball again," recalled Bez. "I went mad at first and complained loudly to Kevin Keegan. However, he wasn't too bothered, he knew what Ginola gave us going forward and that's what mattered to him. As long as the manager was aware of my difficulties and understood it wasn't so bad. But I often wondered what the fans made of me caught in a tidal wave of attacks."

While Ginola did not invent diving – the plague of the continent – he was quite capable of reacting to the slightest hint of boot upon body. Famed writer Salman Rushdie, profiling David in *Le Foot* and referring to his ability to tumble over a tackle, wrote:

"A great diver is like a salmon leaping, twisting, falling. A great dive can last almost as long as the dying of a swan. And it can, of course, influence the referee!"

However, the death of Ginola's international career, just before he came Newcastle United, wasn't down to diving or his lack of work rate but, ironically, to what was normally his greatest strength. He was let down by his passing and hounded not just out of the French national side but effectively out of his native land as well.

David had made his international debut against Albania in November of 1990 and been capped 17 times, but a misplaced back-pass not only cost France a goal but a place in the 1994 World Cup finals in America. He gifted the ball to Bulgaria's Emil Kostadinov, who scored and was castigated for it by luminaries like team-mate Eric Cantona and former Liverpool manager Gerard Houllier, who unbelievably labelled him a "criminal."

A nation was never to forgive, and Ginola never played for France again as they entered a period of domination as World Cup winners and European champions. If David was to suffer personally then England were to gain a crowd-pleaser and ambassador as he turned his gaze over the English Channel – first to Newcastle, and then Spurs where he was a giant in performances.

What Ginola brought with him, apart from creativity, was the ability to score spectacular goals. Two stand out in my memory of his time with United. One in the 5-0 mauling of Manchester United but, even more sensational, a UEFA Cup effort against Hungarian outfit Ferencvaros at St. James's Park.

Both were in his second season at the club, before Christmas when the light went out for David. Manchester United's appearance on Tyneside brought a thirst for revenge for not only had they snatched the championship out of Newcastle's weakening grasp, but they had also humiliated them in the FA Charity Shield at Wembley back in August.

If Darren Peacock's opening goal was a tad controversial (his header just creeping over the line), the Magpies' second in front of a huge, expectant live TV audience brooked no such debate. A brilliant turn by Ginola and cross-shot from the edge of the box flew past Peter Schmeichel. That was the signal for a bean feast. The home United ran riot to triumph 5-0.

The UEFA Cup goal against the Hungarians in October 1996 was sublime in its execution. A clearance winged its way towards Ginola on the edge of the penalty box. In one movement he killed the ball on his chest, took it away from a defender as it dropped onto his thigh, and then volleyed home off the other foot, the ball crashing in off the crossbar.

The BBC later rated it as United's top European goal ever with the citation: "It was the most accomplished piece of skill ever enacted by a Newcastle player."

However, the end was nigh. Ginola was denied a dream move to Spanish giants Barcelona, where his swaggering style of play would have made him a god, but what followed was even worse for him. Keegan had informed the Frenchman that with United charging after honours it was only right for him to stay – and then he subsequently quit himself over the New Year period, ironically following a 7-1 mauling of Tottenham Hotspur and a 3-0 demolition of Leeds United.

Rightly or wrongly Ginola felt betrayed and never again did we witness him at his destructive best in black and white stripes. Whereas Ginola had played in 17 of United's first 18 Premiership matches, he only started another three after Keegan left with four substitute appearances. New manager Kenny Dalglish not only sacrificed Ginola but also sold top scorer Les Ferdinand, both to Tottenham. Ferdie never reached the highs he had at St. James's Park with the cockerel on his chest but Ginola most certainly did.

Some have attempted to compare another French left winger with Ginola, Laurent Robert, who played in Bobby Robson's Newcastle side. However, while Robert had pace and a ferocious free-kick, I frankly think any attempt to bracket them is a huge insult to Ginola. He was the master craftsman.

David became the talk of the Seven Sisters Road, peaking in season 1998-99 when his slalom runs and spectacular strikes earned him both the Football Writers' Association and PFA Player Of The Year awards as Tottenham lifted the Worthington Cup. That sort of blanket recognition of a maverick talent was his official acceptance in English football.

Spurs defeated Leicester City 1-0 at Wembley with only 10 men to lift the League Cup having overcome Manchester United 3-1 in the quarter-finals (Ginola scored) and Liverpool, also by 3-1, at Anfield in the fourth round.

After joining Aston Villa and Everton at the end of his career Ginola moved back to Cote d'Azur in 2002.

Outside of football his presence on the catwalks, appearances in *HELLO!* magazine and on various TV advertisements bracketed him alongside supermodels and led to pop star celebrity status. But his role as an international ambassador for the Red Cross anti-landmines campaign, following the example of Princess Diana, elevated him into serious charity work.

Nethertheless many will recall above most his commercial for *L'Oreal* hair products and David's distinctive Gallic accent as he excused his pampering with the immortal words: "Because I'm worth it."

Having retired from football, what Ginola had to say about how he saw the game and what direction he would take as a manager or coach, was hugely illuminating.

"I would choose to build my team around a very strong spine," he told us. "That means bringing in the best goalkeeper, the best central defender, the best central midfield players and the best striker. The holding midfielders are so important to the team and I would want a partnership such as Patrick Vieira and Emmanuel Petit formed at Arsenal. Two anchormen would then allow the players on the flanks to go up and down and create a threat to the opposition.

"When Franz Beckenbauer arrived at Marseille he said: 'The first thing I will do is build the defence' and I would do the same with my team so I would have an imposing figure like Sol Campbell in it. The striker is very important and they don't come any better than Alan Shearer, a goalscorer who could hold the ball up front.

"When I played at PSG we had George Weah as the main striker with me playing off him. That is the way I wanted to play at Newcastle with Shearer, but it just wasn't to be, and that is the way I would set up my team. I would want players who work with the ball, who can keep it away from the opposition.

"The best managers in the world know that the idea of football is to build the team from the defence. I remember when I played in Paris under Artur George that we got a lot of criticism because we didn't score many goals. But at the end of the season we won the title. If you keep a clean sheet there is always the possibility of you scoring a goal and winning. So I would build from the back and have players like myself up front, that would be very nice!"

That the flamboyant Ginola would choose to build a team around defensive meanness and would have preferred to play on the shoulder of Shearer at Newcastle, rather than on the left wing where he trail-blazed through English soccer, is totally surprising. Keeping it tight and nicking a goal was hardly Keegan's way or what built the reputation of the Entertainers of which Ginola was a sparkling member.

Surprising indeed, but then wasn't everything David Desire Marc Ginola did?

DAVID GINOLA - CAREER STATS	
BORN:	Gassin
DATE OF BIRTH:	January 25 1967
JOINED UNITED:	July 1995
UNITED LEAGUE APPS:	58
GOALS:	6
INT. CAPS (France):	17
GOALS:	3

Alan
Shearer

Alan Shearer walked into deserved retirement well decorated – Newcastle's greatest-ever marksman, the most prolific goalscorer in Premier League history, captain of United and England. A man's man, the last of the English bulldog centre-forwards.

It was entirely appropriate that Wor Jackie Milburn's goalscoring mantle should be passed on to another Geordie. He would have wished it to be so. United love nought better than their own. They are about local lads who become gods. About No. 9s of such prowess that they pass into legend.

Milburn was so revered that a statue of him, right foot cocked like the hammer of a gun, was mounted in the city. Soon it will be joined by one of Big Al.

He sacrificed a shedful of medals to turn his back on the seduction of Manchester United and come home to entertain his own folk. That's a dedication deeply appreciated by those of the faith and is why a sell-out crowd of 52,000 packed St. James's Park for his testimonial.

Shearer insisted that all he had ever wanted to do was to play No. 9 for Newcastle United and for a decade he did so. Every Geordie kid who has kicked a tennis ball around the back lanes that overlook the Tyne will know precisely of those dreams. We all had them. We could shut our eyes and see glory. However, Shearer also touched it and embraced it.

When he finally quit amid tears of joy and emotion in May of 2006 one fan, overcome with what he had been privileged to witness in his lifetime, was moved to write to the *Chronicle*:

"God created the world in seven days, then on Monday he made Alan Shearer." Those of us paid to be wordsmiths could not have bettered it.

Immensely strong and superb at holding the ball up, Shearer's thunderous shot and bullet headers peppered many a keeper into submission. His 206 goals, which took him beyond Wor Jackie's record to the very pinnacle of United's goalscoring charts, stands for every young buck who wants to take aim. However, in today's money-obsessed environment, I wonder if any player will remain loyal enough to one club to overhaul such a mighty figure.

Shearer operated in the minefield that is the penalty area, a back alley of flick knives and muggings rather than long-distance cannon fire. His was the most pressurised of jobs, a place where there is no hiding but much glory for the successful. Shearer was rock hard, a centre-forward who gave as much as he took. Central defenders who played against him couldn't bully him. Fear wasn't an emotion he recognised.

Nevertheless we ought to be truthful and when Shearer came home instead of heading off to Manchester United, he did so not only because of his heritage but because he also expected medals over the next 10 years. Of course he did – United had just finished runners-up in the championship and, mighty superstars already aboard, were poised to end a drought dating back to 1969. With England's finest to add his ravenous appetite for goals, surely the long wait would soon be over.

The only trouble is that football is a team game and while Shearer never ever let anyone down, others most certainly sold us short. He was cheated as we were all cheated.

Oh, the Magpies went very close – but not close enough. Second, third and fourth in the Premier League, two FA Cup finals plus two semi-finals, UEFA Cup semi-final, second group phase of the Champions League. All decent stuff but inevitably short of ultimate glory.

Throughout 395 games and another nine as a sub, Shearer straight of back and head held high, waged war on behalf of Newcastle and never shirked a challenge.

Of course, he was always destined to be a star. The surprise was that it would appear only Jack Hixon, a British rail worker and part-time scout, recognised the fact immediately. Jack couldn't have sent a young Alan further from home, down to the south coast but, at 17 years of age making his debut for Southampton in top-flight football, Shearer scored a hat-trick and suddenly everyone knew what we had.

His ability to plunder goals by the sackload was the major factor in small-town club Blackburn Rovers capturing the Premier League championship – Shearer's only winner's medal. Jack Walker's millions were never more wisely spent. And Newcastle hardly wasted a world record £15m either – their poor return was down to others. What we got was gilt edged, a physical battering ram of a leader whose body took terrible punishment on behalf of his club.

Shearer scored three hat-tricks for United plus a five-goal haul in an astonishing 8-0 victory over Sheffield Wednesday. He also took Newcastle to the 1998 FA Cup final at Wembley, scoring the goal that beat Sheffield United and a year later notched the two that defeated Spurs in the semis. Same old Shearer, always scoring!

Perhaps we were all surprised that he changed his mind – something previously unknown – and stayed on for an extra season. It proved to be a struggle at times with Michael Owen only fleetingly a companion, the manager sacked, and goals generally in short supply across the whole spectrum of the team.

Ancient legs perhaps didn't respond as quickly as the brain

and while Shearer remained supreme in the air, clever of thought and as physically challenging as ever, his movement was naturally more restricted.

We prayed the season would bring him the going away present of a medal but an early defeat at Wigan Athletic ended Carling Cup hopes and a draw to play Chelsea away in the quarter-finals of the FA Cup determined that there would be no fairytale ending.

However, for everyone who was inside St. James's Park when Alan eventually put daylight between himself and Wor Jackie Milburn's two ton of goals, the moment was worth the wait. Emotion poured down the terraces and engulfed Shearer in sheer love.

It was appropriate that the goal should come at home, should come in open play rather than from the penalty spot and should come at his favourite Gallowgate End. Portsmouth were the victims on February 4, 2006 – a date to be remembered. United won 2-0 and young Charles N'Zogbia had the honour of scoring Newcastle's other goal.

Not unnaturally, indeed quite appropriately, Shearer scored too on his very last appearance in black and white, though he was taking his curtain call three matches early. A penalty to put the Magpies ahead for the first time sparked a hugely satisfying 4-1 win at Sunderland before Shearer collapsed under a heavy challenge and, knee busted, hobbled into history.

Top of the pile, he leads a distinguished list of 10 great black and white goalscorers which reads:

1 Alan Shearer   206 goals, 404 games;
2 Jackie Milburn   200 goals, 397 games;
3 Len White   153 goals, 270 games;
4 Hughie Gallacher   143 goals, 174 games;
5 Malcolm Macdonald   121 goals, 228 games;
6 Peter Beardsley   119 goals, 325 games;

7 Tom McDonald	113 goals, 367 games;
8 Bobby Mitchell	113 goals, 410 games;
9 Neil Harris	101 goals, 194 games;
10 Bryan Pop Robson	97 goals, 243 games.

That Shearer was forever a scoring machine can best be determined by another set of figures – his career record away from St. James's Park. It reads thus:

Southampton (1987-1992):	148 apps, 38 goals;
Blackburn Rovers (1992-1996)	170 apps, 130 goals;
England (1992-2000):	63 apps, 30 goals;
England B and U21:	13 apps, 13 goals.

One of the finest centre-forwards this country has ever produced, Shearer will stand shoulder-to-shoulder with Wor Jackie as long as history books record great feats. Whereas Milburn spent his whole career at St. James's Park after scoring six goals in a trial match, no-one at Newcastle foresaw what a young Shearer would become and off he went to score goals for fun at Southampton from a hat-trick debut at 17 against Arsenal and win a championship at Blackburn, before a then world record fee of £15m brought him home to start from scratch again.

Shearer became the Magpie who thieved goals for 10 seasons during which time his exploits led to him becoming England skipper, reaching 30 goals for his country in the process.

Wor Jackie and Big Al were precisely the same and totally different. Both Geordies, both modest and model professionals. Both centre-forwards and monumental goalscorers.

However, Milburn was exceptionally quick and Shearer wasn't. Alternatively Jackie wasn't too clever in the air whereas our modern-day hero was as good as Douglas Bader when flying the clouds.

Jackie only scored in two competitions for Newcastle, the Football League and the FA Cup, because in the 1940s and 50s there were no new-fangled trophies. Alan, on the other hand, stretched his bulls' eyes across the Premier League, FA Cup, League Cup, Champions League, UEFA Cup and Intertoto Cup.

The respect great men have for one another became apparent when Shearer took his testimonial night against Celtic. Wor Jackie's widow Laura was in the stand as Alan's guest to share a proud moment and further tribute was paid to Ashington's finest on the advertising hoardings each side of the halfway line.

I've always been fascinated with Newcastle's No. 9 folk heroes and privileged to indulge that fascination. I filmed a TV documentary not so long ago on Hughie Gallacher, spoke at the family's commemorative service for Wor Jackie in Ashington, was best man at Malcolm Macdonald's wedding and had Alan Shearer come to my rescue with a sell-out evening at St. James's Park to raise money for Gateshead when I was the chairman and we were in dire financial need. Those are memories that will accompany me to the grave. These sort of players only come along occasionally and are to be treasured for the countless hours of pleasure they gave.

Of course, Alan's new record doesn't airbrush Milburn out of United's picture. That would be insulting as well as downright stupid to suggest. Just as it would be ridiculous to state in years to come when a new young gun comes along that Shearer is no more. What we need to do is enjoy every single one of the centre-forward superstars in their own right.

It is entirely appropriate that Shearer's mentor Jack Hixon should have witnessed all No. 9 legends. Because of his 86 years on this planet he is one of the few people alive to have actually seen Gallacher play, to have loved Wor Jackie, gawped at the plundering pace of SuperMac, and physically put Shearer on the road to fame and fortune.

"Hughie was tiny but a real firebrand and a devastating centre-forward," Jack told me. "Wor Jackie was fast enough to catch pigeons, the epitome of a local hero. SuperMac was also lightning and so powerful he carried Burnley's centre-half on his back to score in the semi-final of the FA Cup. However, for me – and I know I'm biased – Shearer was the best of the lot. A colossus of a player and of a person."

Jack, a grand old man with a fund of vivid memories and a meticulous brain, adores Alan and recalls their early days with the fondness a father has for a favourite son.

"When I approached his dad to see if Alan could go to Southampton, an awful long way away from Newcastle, I was told to ask the lad himself. 'He'll make up his mind,' smiled Mr. Shearer. I remember that at 14 I put Alan on a coach in the centre of Newcastle bound for the south coast. He was all by himself, had to change in London and then go to Southampton. Hours upon hours it would take. Was I worried? No, not a bit. If anyone on the bus needed any help they only had to ask Alan and he would have looked after them!"

Hixon chortles at the story because it typified the maturity of Shearer even in the earliest of his teen years. So did his response on the field. "When he played his first game on trial at Southampton he scored five goals and held up all four fingers and thumb on his right hand. That's how confident he was."

Never out of touch with one another from that day to this, Jack adds: "Alan might not suffer fools gladly but he's as loyal as the day is long. It is a trait that never waivers. He is a friend for life. What he has made of himself is not down to me but to his single-mindedness, talent and driving force. He will be a success at whatever he chooses to do and that includes being a football manager at some time in the future. Of that I have absolutely no doubt."

Most managers deeply appreciate special talent and work diligently to get the ultimate out of such players. Kevin Keegan bought Shearer because he recognised true quality and Sir Bobby Robson told me upon his appointment that his No. 1 job was to get Alan onside. Robson made a deliberate effort and the result was instant – Shearer notched not one, not a hat-trick but FIVE against Sheffield Wednesday in Bobby's first match at St. James's Park.

Great marksmen live by goals as we live by fresh air and so when rookie striker Paul Robinson, on as a sub, asked if he could take a second penalty with Shearer on four goals and United on seven, he received a withering look which could have curdled milk. No words were needed.

Matt Le Tissier, a wonderful ball player who devoted his life to Southampton, recalled the single-mindedness of Shearer when talking about the Geordie lad's debut in April of 1988.

"I was dropped to the reserves so Shearer could make his full debut for Southampton and he scored a hat-trick against Arsenal," recalled Le Tiss. "'Christ' I thought, 'how am I going to get back in the team?' If ever a player made the most of his ability it was Shearer."

Keegan and Robson – co-incidentally United's most successful managers since Joe Harvey won in Europe – recognised the worth of their line leader but Ruud Gullit did not. A majestic forward himself, he refused to accept Shearer's stature, made it personal and lost the battle.

Having dismissed Newcastle v Sunderland as not a real derby because the two clubs weren't from the same city – sacrilege in Toon Army eyes – Gullit proceeded to axe Shearer and Duncan Ferguson, leaving them stranded and squirming on the sub's bench playing a kid, Robinson, up front on his own. Robinson had even admitted in the club programme that if he scored against Sunderland he would shed a tear because he was a Mackem. I ask you, what were United's faithful to think!

Presumably to gain maximum impact Gullit never told Shearer he was dropped, the first time it had ever happened to him, incidentally. He merely pinned up the team sheet and allowed Alan to join the queue searching for information!

When the team filtered into the Press room it was greeted with total disbelief. A suicide note would not have been clearer. As a statement of intent there was only one outcome. On a night as foul as the Geordies' mood Newcastle lost 2-1 and all was over.

The following morning Shearer drove straight to the training ground to confront Gullit only to discover he had been beaten to the punch. Big Dunc had got there before him and the door was off its hinges!

Gullit had attempted to rid United of Shearer, prove he wasn't needed and get him out of the dressing room, and lost a huge gamble. He fell upon his sword.

The Dutchman had also fingered Rob Lee, Shearer's big mate, kicking him out of the team and even refusing him a squad number. Rob watched the fateful derby from the stands but upon the appointment of Robson both Shearer and Lee were immediately restored to duty with considerable effect. A Friday night spent in Shearer's bedroom in a London city-centre hotel saw a crafty Robson plot his way to success around the presence of England's finest.

United lost by a single goal to Chelsea but then came home and knocked Wednesday into the middle of next week. Another period of joy and excitement was about to dawn. Third place in the Premiership and wonderful Champions League nights across Europe beckoned.

In a special season, 2002-03, United reached the pinnacle of Robson's regime finishing third in the league and reaching the second group stage of Europe's finest competition, the very brink of the last eight of the Champions League.

Most Toonies will consider the last-gasp victory against Feyenoord in the De Kuip Stadium when Craig Bellamy sent temperatures soaring as United's greatest moment, but there was also a significant match in Group Stage 2 that heralded Newcastle's new-found stature. They travelled to Inter Milan accompanied by 10,000 boisterous Geordies to shake the San Siro to its very foundations.

The Magpies outplayed the ill-tempered Italians for long periods and deservedly went in front when Shearer converted Bellamy's run and cross. Vieri equalised but Shearer was on the spot again to fire home after Laurent Robert's fierce cross caused mayhem. A Cordoba goal settled the contest at 2-2 but United had proved beyond doubt through Shearer's brace that they could compete as equals with Europe's elite.

Some men are destined to stand apart, heroes who become legends and are thus secured in history for life and beyond. Alan Shearer is one of those men.

ALAN SHEARER - CAREER STATS	
BORN:	Gosforth
DATE OF BIRTH:	August 13 1970
JOINED UNITED:	December 1994
UNITED LEAGUE APPS:	301
GOALS:	148
INT. CAPS (England):	63
GOALS:	30

1995-1997

Les
Ferdinand

Big, bold and handsome, Les Ferdinand looked the epitome of a centre-forward. Nicknamed Sir Les, he had a regal presence which Geordie fans loved and took to their hearts.

How good was he? Kevin Keegan not only spent £6m on him when that was a club record fee but once he took Andy Cole in his car to Liverpool to watch "the complete centre-forward" in action. And Alan Shearer called Ferdie "my perfect partner." Considering that the likes of Teddy Sheringham, Chris Sutton, Peter Beardsley, Michael Owen, Duncan Ferguson and Craig Bellamy performed at Shearer's shoulder, the compliment was Everest huge.

His signing was eventually clinched in June of 1995 with chief executive Freddie Fletcher admitting: "Some transfers are completed in a flash but this one took 18 months. We almost got Les twice before it was all done and dusted. I seemed to spend most of my time contacting Richard Thompson at QPR lodging Ferdinand bids. We had a £5.5m offer on the table but Aston Villa upped the price to £6m and were given permission to talk to him. It was now clear cut – we either matched Villa or forgot about it."

Keegan revealed: "I always held up Les as the complete centre-forward. One day I was climbing into my car at St. James's Park to go and watch Ferdinand play for QPR at Liverpool. Andy Cole just happened to be going in to collect his mail and I yelled: 'Andy what are you doing tonight?' Before he knew what was happening he was sitting next to me on his way to Merseyside! Cole was scoring an awful lot of goals for us but I told him I wanted him just to watch Les play – no-one else. To see how he led his line, his appreciation of players around him, and his team work. Andy, a young player, could learn from that.

"At the time I wanted Ferdinand to play alongside Cole but in the end he was the striker I brought in to take over Andy's mantle. Sometimes perseverance is the name of the game."

Cole's sale to Manchester United, after smashing the Newcastle goalscoring record was so controversial that even Keegan, much loved, had to face bewildered fans on the steps of St. James's Park demanding an explanation. Kevin's answer was for the supporters to trust him and back him. Their reward was to be Ferdie.

Peter Beardsley, who played in harness with both Cole and Ferdinand, gave me his perspective on Keegan's bravery. "It was a colossal decision which shook everyone at the time but, frankly, I can understand it. Andy was unbelievable in the season he scored a record 41 goals – I don't think that feat will ever be beaten in the Premiership – but by the time the second season came round he wasn't the same player. I don't know if it was boredom or what but it was a different Cole.

"Les, who eventually came in for him, was a class act. The best header of the ball I ever saw bar none. Sometimes you don't realise how good a player is until you play with him."

Whereas Cole has been an introvert, a man who appeared at first impression to be arrogant and aloof when in reality painfully shy, Ferdie was the exact opposite in nature and that bore him in good stead on Tyneside. Geordies love their heroes to be larger than life.

A Cockney of St. Lucian parents, Les was 28-years-old and at the peak of his career. Like Warren Barton, bought in the same week, he had began playing non-League football but had smashed 100 goals for QPR and Turkish side Besiktas by the time Keegan prised him away.

However, there was a deserved windfall for Hayes, his last non-League club. They received £600,000 of the £6m fee Newcastle paid because of a sell-on clause they inserted when Ferdie joined QPR – a shrewd piece of business that netted them a huge sum for a non-League club.

His debut at the beginning of the 1995-96 season was beautifully scripted – home to Coventry City in the sun. United roared to a 3-0 victory capped by a Ferdinand finish at the Gallowgate End. "When I scored, the place erupted," he later recalled. "I can't remember having a better feeling on a football pitch."

Football's newly-crowned Entertainers smashed their way to the top of the Premiership with Ferdie, barrel chested and brave, notching 16 times in his first 13 games. Geordieland began dreaming of a championship never won since 1927, so long ago (69 years) that virtually no supporter could remember it.

With Keith Gillespie (bought as part of the Cole deal) and David Ginola supplying a bombardment of crosses from the wings, and Peter Beardsley and Rob Lee the midfield back-up, Ferdie was rampant. During the months of September and October he bagged 12 goals in eight consecutive matches. When Wimbledon came to town Les clinched a hat-trick in a soaraway 6-1 victory. However, football never allows complacency. If the sun is out, however brilliantly, rain is always around the next corner and as Christmas came and went Ferdie and Newcastle faltered in their magnificent stride.

This was the season when famously a 12-point lead was blown to Manchester United and one of the reasons was that Ferdinand was carrying a hip injury. He manfully fought on but his great frame was badly wounded. Whereas he had scored 21 goals in his first 22 league and cup matches, he managed only eight in his last 22. The stars around him simultaneously dimmed as Alex Ferguson's men crept closer and closer and Tino Asprilla, bought from Parma in Italy for £7.5m, failed to become an instant hit at Ferdie's side.

Many trace back Newcastle's championship failure to the match at St. James's Park when Peter Schmeichel was magnificent, saving twice when Ferdie looked certain to net. Then in the second half up popped Eric Cantona to snatch a winner. As the title race came to boiling point the Magpies fatally faltered in three crucial away fixtures – the famous 3-4 defeat at Liverpool in the Premiership's "Match of the Decade", at Blackburn and Nottingham Forest. All three times Newcastle had led but, obsessive attackers, were caught on the counter at the back.

Despite this Ferdinand finished his first season in black and white with 29 goals and the affection of a crowd which loved barnstorming leaders, fleet of foot, dangerous in the air and courageous beyond the call of duty. If Andy Cole had done much to kill off any lingering racist elements on Tyneside then Ferdie made certain such evil was never to raise its head again.

Keegan, destroyed by his championship failure, pulled together a bruised ego and battered body to find Ferdinand the greatest of partners during the close season. Inevitably KK was more concerned about the attack than defence, which has cost him most, and his answer was to splash a world record £15m on England's magnificent line-leader Alan Shearer.

There were those away from the banks of the Tyne who immediately suggested the two could never play together. Both were essentially No. 9s. Both strong target men, both deadly in the air and neither likely to give ground. How wrong they were. If Laurel dovetailed with Hardy, Morecambe needed Wise and fish never came without chips then Shearer and Ferdinand were a partnership made in black and white heaven. How defenders hated to be faced with such an awesome

physical challenge from two hit men, combined cost £21m. An hour-and-a-half of non-stop buffeting into submission.

They took time to refine their act but when they did they were dynamite. Between them they scored 49 goals despite both being injured for some considerable period.

Shearer, inevitably, netted on his home debut against Wimbledon and then Ferdie knocked home the winner in the last derby match played at Roker Park as United triumphed 2-1 over Sunderland. Les cracked a header from Ginola's corner with pace and precision. Off went United in search of that elusive championship with six wins in six starts and 10 goals for the "Dynamic Duo", Batman and Robin. As Newcastle and their fans gorged themselves Sir Les rattled in eight goals in six matches and Shearer six in seven.

However, the highlight was undoubtedly when Manchester United came back having nicked the Geordies' crown. They were literally slaughtered 5-0 in what was a classic encounter when every single Entertainer in Newcastle colours displayed their full repertoire. Of course, Shearer and Ferdie were awesome in tandem, both getting on the scoresheet and Ginola hit an exquisite cross-shot. But the goal treasured by every member of the Toon Army was Philippe Albert's sumptuous chip over a stranded Schmeichel. Oh I can feel the warm glow all over again!

At the very moment when once again the Toon Army smelled the title the wheels came off. First Shearer was sidelined with a persistent groin injury and then his partner sustained a depressed fracture of the cheekbone as well as other niggles. They missed almost a dozen matches each and with them went United's cutting edge and their dreams.

If that was not bad enough, the whole of Tyneside was rocked in the January when Keegan, the architect of the modern United, sensationally quit amid mystery, anger and despair. The suggestion was that he took to his heels after a disagreement over the direction of the club as it moved to PLC status. But to this day people are disappointed and perplexed by his actions. Certainly players as well as fans had a right to feel let down by the suddenness of it all. Ginola had stayed purely because of KK, Shearer had just arrived having snubbed Manchester United but was now deserted by the man he put his faith in and Beardsley had been the greatest of Keegan believers. Shearer admitted to being "devastated" though Ferdie noted, with hindsight that "the boss had been acting strangely."

While one section of the board was courting Bobby Robson at Barcelona another was talking to Kenny Dalglish. Robson pulled out at the news all were apparently not of the same mind, though he was to arrive later, and so Dalglish was unveiled. A fabulous footballer who had won the Premiership with Shearer at Blackburn but who was in many ways the very opposite to Keegan. Whereas KK was a one-man PR machine, bubbly and bright with both Press and public, Dalglish was dour outside of the dressing room.

The fans found the difference hard to stomach and, sure enough, the rest of the 1996-97 season was something of an anti-climax. For Ferdinand it was to end with dire consequences.

United slipped from the head of the Premiership table but recovered to finish as runners-up for the second season in a row and qualify for the new Champions League. Shearer top-scored with 28 goals and Ferdinand weighed in with 21 more. Proof, you might say, that the two were a huge success together. Shearer certainly thought so but, apparently, Dalglish did not.

The summer break was awash with speculation that Dalglish was prepared to offload Ferdie, by now 30-years-old, and reshape his side around Shearer. The manager considered two big men together a luxury and the outcome was to be hugely to Newcastle's disadvantage.

When a bid of £6m dropped on Dalglish's desk form Spurs his

fate was sealed. It was back to London for a player who, in only two seasons, had captured hearts forever. Off to White Hart Lane where he would play once again with Ginola, also sold by Dalglish.

"I was told the transfer was for financial reasons," said Les. "But I was under no illusions. Kenny Dalglish was the manager and I knew that if he had said his team, as it stood, would win the championship the board would have kept me. I would love to have stayed longer because I had a tremendous relationship with the supporters, and still have, but I was deprived of the chance."

The huge irony of it all was that on the very day Ferdinand was in London to sign for Tottenham, Shearer fractured his tibia, badly ruptured ankle ligaments and displaced a joint in a pre-season match at Goodison Park. In a blind panic, United attempted to halt the Ferdie transfer but were too late and, from possessing two of the most formidable strikers in English football, they suddenly had neither. Perhaps Dalglish deserved such luck for his crass stupidity in selling off such an asset but the Toon Army certainly did not, and they suffered too.

Those brought in by a manager never liked by his supporters, Jon Dahl Tomasson and Temuri Ketsbaia, were a pale shadow of Shearer and Ferdinand. Neither was an orthodox centre-forward and a desperate Dalglish, looking around for help, plunged for a couple of his old Liverpool team-mates in Ian Rush and John Barnes. In their pomp the cream of the crop but now with one foot in the grave. Next came Andreas Andersson, who played in an Alice band and looked more like a blonde cheerleader than a hard-nosed striker. Oh, the mess, the ruinous break-up of Keegan's squad.

Ferdinand had won the PFA Player of the Year award in his opening season with United, the first Magpie to do so, and received his trophy from Pele, no less. Now he was at Tottenham where he remained for six seasons, but never achieved what he did in black and white stripes. Often hampered by injury, he moved across London to help West Ham United in January of 2003, then on to Leicester City. Following their relegation he signed for Bolton Wanderers in July 2004, extending his Premiership career at the age of 38 before a final hurrah at Reading.

Ferdie can boast a career record of 465 games and 189 goals, plus 17 caps for England and five goals with the three lions bouncing on a broad chest. Surprisingly, in my view, after an extremely successful opening season with United when they almost captured the Premier League championship, he never saw any action in Euro '96 despite making the England squad.

Les's reputation with every Geordie is such that whenever he returned to St. James's Park he received the sort of warm ovation previously reserved down the years for the likes of Hughie Gallacher and SuperMac, two No. 9 legends.

He may never have been knighted by the Queen – just the fans – but he did receive the MBE in 2005 and his name lives on within the game through his cousins, Rio and Anton Ferdinand. His son Aaron actually followed dad's path into non-League soccer. A qualified helicopter pilot, Les Ferdinand has always flown high and handsome.

LES FERDINAND - CAREER STATS	
BORN:	Paddington
DATE OF BIRTH:	December 18 1966
JOINED UNITED:	July 1995
UNITED LEAGUE APPS:	68
GOALS:	41
INT. CAPS (England):	17
GOALS:	5

1997-

Shay
Given

If Kevin Keegan's Entertainers are the symbol of what every Newcastle fan wishes to see in his team – style and flair most of all – then they are a decent yardstick by which to judge others. That being so, Shay Given can preen himself with some justification.

The splendid Rob Lee left me in no doubt when we were talking of bygone days that in his opinion only Shay from United's 2006-07 squad would get in Keegan's all-star side. And Peter Beardsley was quick to add his seal of approval, while also making a case for Nobby Solano on his form during his first stay with Newcastle.

If United have not always been well served by their custodians then Given is a magnificent exception. A wonderfully agile shot-stopper who amongst his considerable attributes can list loyalty, a commodity not always in ready supply in a world dominated by obscene amounts of money. Like Alan Shearer, his willingness to sacrifice medals elsewhere for the adulation and appreciation of Geordies who regularly fill St. James's Park is a trait to be treasured.

If staying put eventually gained Shearer the club's goalscoring record then perhaps Shay will be rewarded by a record himself – for his number of appearances. At the moment, appropriately perhaps, that record is in the hands of another legendary keeper Jimmy Lawrence, who played 496 competitive games for

United, a staggering 432 of them in the league. As the summer of 2007 brought temporary respite for our pro footballers Given's grand total, restricted by three lengthy spells injured that season, was 413 – and at 31 years of age he can go on to challenge Lawrence, especially operating in a position where careers stretch way beyond those of outfield players.

Lawrence is from a world apart of course, straddling the First World War which ripped a hole in his figures. The Scot joined United in 1904 when keepers wore the same jerseys as the rest of the team and the offside law had not been remodelled, and he eventually retired in 1922. He was the last line of defence in all Newcastle's Edwardian successes – three championships and five FA Cup finals, which no one in black and white is ever going to top.

Given is the best shot-stopper in the Premiership and probably has to be because, despite officially being listed as 6ft tall, he is not big for a modern-day keeper. Therefore on crosses, getting above a melee of bodies can provide a challenge. He is more Ronnie Simpson than Peter Schmeichel.

A fabulous career emanated from the most risky of beginnings. A young footballer anxious to make his way in an uncertain world, Given first turned down Alex Ferguson and then walked out on Glasgow Celtic. Mind-blowing it most certainly was, but if you are from the south of Ireland where these two clubs are revered above all others, it's almost sacrilege. But then Shay was not a young man who followed the traditional or conventional path.

He only turned his affections from Gaelic Football to Association Football because there wasn't a living to be had at that peculiarly Irish sport. Even so, he wanted to play outfield and be the scorer of spectacular goals, only becoming a keeper because his dad insisted that strikers were "ten a penny" while goalies were special.

Fair enough, but how on earth can a youngster turn down

Man United? Or tell Celtic to jump through their own hoops because he wasn't going to? Easy, it would appear.

Shay was playing for his local side Lifford Celtic who in 1992 reached the last four of the FAI Junior Cup from a starting line-up of 1,200 clubs.

"Scouts were taking a lot of notice and I actually went over to Manchester United for two weeks," Given told me. "Alex Ferguson was really good with me. I could have signed but my dad suggested that I might have a better chance of breaking through at Celtic. They had a lot of pulling power with me. Liam Brady, their manager at the time, is an Irish legend of course and their keeper Packie Bonner was my hero."

Two years' apprenticeship followed at Celtic Park after which, Brady having departed, so did Given – to work on his dad's pitch and putt course.

"Lou Macari became manager and he offered me a contract, but it was nowhere near what I wanted," explained Shay. "I'd grafted hard without reward so my dad told me to come back home and I worked during the summer on the pitch and putt course we'd built on the site of our market garden centre."

Ironically it was a Celtic legend, Kenny Dalglish, who took advantage of his old club's meanness. Aged 18, Shay was to join Dalglish at Blackburn Rovers on a free transfer. Next time Kenny called it cost him and Newcastle United £1.5m.

In an age when there are more agents in football than a James Bond film, Given didn't possess a 20 per cent man. Instead his dad Seamus did all his deals for nowt. Oh, and that name – Given Jnr ended up with exactly the same moniker as dad, Seamus John Given, so when they inevitably became known as "big Seamus and wee Seamus" son's handle was shortened from Seamus to Shay. It made life easier.

Given spent more time on loan than a library book when he was at Blackburn. With Tim Flowers barring his way Shay became the 'yo-yo man' going out on loan three separate times.

His spells in exile were at Swindon Town (twice) and Sunderland, where he became a terrace hero who was eventually lost to bitter rivals Newcastle amid much wailing and beating of breast. The day the loan stranger road into town heralded success for both Swindon and Sunderland. Shay conceded just one goal in five games at the start of the 1995-96 season, which laid the foundations for Swindon's eventual Second Division title and at Sunderland, he kept 12 clean sheets in 17 First Division appearances to help guarantee them promotion.

"I got a championship medal with Sunderland but nothing with Swindon because I hadn't played enough games," explained Given. "There was talk I would sign for Sunderland on a permanent basis but to be truthful once Newcastle came in it was a different story. So much about them appealed to me more – they were second in the Premier League, were in the European Champions League, had fabulous support and were managed by my old boss Kenny Dalglish. It was all far too much to turn down.

"Blackburn offered me a three or four-year contract with a lot better wages but it wasn't about money. They couldn't guarantee me first-team football and that's what I really wanted. I've never ever regretted making that decision."

Given signed for United on July 14, 1997 and played in the FA Cup final against Arsenal at the end of his first season. That was for Dalglish, of course, but a year later, 1999, when Newcastle once again trod the holy turf of Wembley, it was with Shay's big rival Steve Harper between the posts. Despite playing in every round en route to the biggest of days Ruud Gullit dropped Shay and went with the older, but more inexperienced Harper as Manchester United chased the treble. It was only Harps' 10th senior match and against the cream who went on to memorably win the European Cup. Newcastle, of course, lost both finals convincingly.

Early on Harper challenged Given for the No. 1 job before Shay emerged as the long-term winner. Steve, a wonderfully steady performer, has been as devoted to black and white as Shay and they have produced a great final barrier for Newcastle over recent years. When chairman of Gateshead I actually signed a young Harper on loan from United after Kevin Keegan scrapped the reserve team and he had nowhere to go. We did the deal in the café at Washington Services and Harps gained extra experience playing in the Conference rather than just sitting on his backside on matchdays.

Given's career had lift off in 2001-02 when he emerged to perform in every Premier League match and was named in the PFA Premiership team of the season. Thus in full flight, Shay was two seasons later the holder of the Premier League record for consecutive appearances, a record later surrendered to Frank Lampard, and by the end of 2005-06 he had incredibly missed only two Premier League games for United in five seasons racking up his 400th career appearance at Middlesbrough on April 9.

Admittedly, once early doors in his United career Given had actually done the unthinkable and asked for a transfer when, fit again, he didn't immediately replace Harper. But he admitted that it was a knee-jerk reaction greatly regretted, and hurriedly rescinded.

Inevitably along the way international longevity went hand-in-hand with permanent residency between the posts for a top Premiership club. Shay, who had a great World Cup in Japan and South Korea, became United's most capped international on April 30, 2003 when he won his 41st cap for the Republic of Ireland (50th in total) whilst at St. James's Park, overtaking Alf McMichael's previous record.

Many have been the memorable matches and milestones Shay has experienced along his personal highway. The stunning 3-2 Champions League victory over Barcelona when Tino

Asprilla notched a hat-trick, similar European victories over Juventus 1-0 and Feyenoord away 3-2 as well as four FA Cup runs – two to Wembley finals and two semis, one played at Wembley and the other at Cardiff's Millennium Stadium.

No doubt Given takes great pride in keeping a clean sheet against the Juve superstars, as indeed he should, and would also recall with pleasure the derby act of defiance that got him shortlisted for 'Save of the Decade' – a spectacular leap to his left to turn away Kevin Phillips' goal-bound shot in the Tyne-Wear encounter at Sunderland in February of 2002.

However, I cannot help but love to wallow in the dramatic victory that cut Barca down to mere mortals in 1997 because it was one of the truly great European nights at St. James's Park watched by a capacity crowd and 200 million on TV around the world. Asprilla was sensational, the hero of course, but the whole night was tinglingly awesome and to be privileged to take part in it, as Shay was, must be something to treasure.

Even without the injured Alan Shearer Newcastle totally destroyed the Spanish champions for an hour with Tino and winger Keith Gillespie running riot. Asprilla's first was from the penalty spot but his second and third goals owed much to the blinding pace of Gillespie, who roasted Spanish international full-back Sergi twice to deliver precision crosses for Tino to spring high and head past Hesp.

Newcastle's work rate took its toll as the match wore on and Barca showed their undoubted talent. First Luis Enrique pulled a goal back and then Figo hit the net two minutes from time but it was too late. Given and his comrades ended winners and heroes every one of them.

Buried amongst all his cherished moments with the Magpies, however, there is one embarrassing incident I suspect Shay would dearly like to overlook. The day an Irishman didn't know where Dublin was! Shay became the man who launched a thousand quips when the Republic's finest got conned by Dion

Dublin at Coventry City.

"It was the most bizarre goal I've ever let in," smiled Given. "I had back-pedalled to take a cross. No one challenged me and I didn't realise Dion Dublin was behind me. I was looking up field and dropped the ball at my feet to kick it clear. I knew I had six seconds and was just preparing to clear when Dublin nipped round on my blind side and kicked the ball into the net. For a moment I thought I might get away with it because the referee, who was anticipating my clearance, ran over to the linesman.

"However, unfortunately, he had seen everything and the goal stood. The gaffer, Kenny Dalglish wasn't too pleased about it afterwards. I've looked over both shoulders ever since!"

That was an isolated aberration, of course, and in the main Given has been a rock in a floundering sea. Such has been the frailty of United's back four on occasions that Shay was sufficiently moved to accuse them of "defending like a pub team" after one particularly embarrassing performance. That, like Shearer, he has given 10 years of service without a winner's medal to show for his loyalty is a disgrace. However, unlike Alan, there is still time for Shay to be rewarded, please God!

Sir Bobby Robson managed Given at Newcastle and later came into contact with him again as Steve Staunton's aide with the Republic of Ireland. He has no doubt about Shay's ability, saying:

"I don't think there is anyone better in the Premiership – or in Europe for that matter. He is one of the most reliable keepers I've ever worked with and he is a phenomenal shot-stopper. Shay got better and better when I was at Newcastle and he has continued to develop.

"The thing that has always impressed me is his consistency, which is what is required to become a genuinely top keeper. Some are absolutely outstanding one match and then a disaster the next, but not him."

Praise indeed, and echoed by Shearer himself, who adds:

"What people don't see is the work Shay does on the training ground. You get out of football what you put in – I've known him from an early age when I was at Blackburn and he's the best there is."

Such is the stature he has attained during his lengthy service with United that when Shearer was forced to retire a few games early because of an injury sustained at Sunderland, Shay had the privilege of skippering the team. And for season 2006-07 he was officially named vice-captain, a rare accolade for a goalkeeper.

The Republic were to follow United's lead. With regular skipper Robbie Keane suspended they turned to Given to lead them out against Slovakia on a historic occasion at Croke Park in March 2007. Appropriate, indeed, because that very night Shay equalled the 80-cap record of his boyhood hero Packie Bonner. He did it in the style he would have wished, too, with a clean sheet and victory. See, nice guys do win!

SHAY GIVEN - CAREER STATS	
BORN:	Lifford
DATE OF BIRTH:	April 20 1976
JOINED UNITED:	July 1997
UNITED LEAGUE APPS:	313
GOALS:	0
INT. CAPS (Rep. of Ireland):	80
GOALS:	0

AWAY FROM THE SPOTLIGHT

Kevin Keegan

Kevin Keegan may have run away to join the circus, but he can't escape the legacy he left behind at Newcastle United.

Keegan, always an enthusiastic all-or-nothing participant in life, has moved his family up to Glasgow to meet his next challenge head-on. The building of a new empire Soccer Circus, an interactive challenge in which the paying public are rewarded for the completion of different skills. Aged 56, it no doubt appeals to the child in him.

However, when Keegan broke off from showing the Jocks how to play soccer, having agreed to a rare interview about a world he no longer wishes to inhabit, he was full of warm nostalgia for The Entertainers, his own collection of ball jugglers and acrobats who stormed the Premier League and captured millions of hearts in the early and mid-1990s.

Indeed, Keegan believes that had his United side won the Premiership, as they oh so nearly did, it would have changed the face of football forever and banished the clawing fear that is stifling our cash-obsessed national game. The shackles, he maintains, would have been thrown off to the benefit of all who care.

A decade has passed since Keegan sensationally walked out on his greatest managerial achievement in January of 1997, but the public wide and far have not forgotten his Newcastle.

"Even now, up here in Glasgow, people approach me to say

they loved that Newcastle team," he told me. "They became besotted with the way we played. So many folk from all over the place tell me they used to travel to St. James's Park to watch us, or sat glued in front of the box. You never see that sort of soccer now with the possible exception of Manchester United. Football today is not my type of football.

"I was new to management at the beginning of the nineties and I thought all football should be played our way. I built a side to play the way I liked the game to be played.

"We didn't go for a team of defenders. We went out to entertain a Geordie public who crave entertainment and that required players of flair and imagination who dared to perform in a certain way. My side and the Geordie fans were a marriage made in heaven.

"Teams are usually all about defence. All the coaching manuals tell you to build from the back, that if you don't concede a goal you can't lose. I preferred to believe that if you didn't score you couldn't win. We were in the entertainment business and I had a simple philosophy. I had no preconceived ideas, no fear of failure. I bought some wonderful players who were adored by the Geordies – Philippe Albert, David Ginola, Peter Beardsley, Rob Lee, Andy Cole, Les Ferdinand, Alan Shearer and, yes, Tino Asprilla. They were priceless, every one of them a wonderful asset.

"We almost achieved the impossible, winning the championship with a squad built on pure football. We should have won it and had we it would not only have changed Newcastle United for good, but all of football. Coaches would have been encouraged to go down our path, to rid us of a negativity that is stifling our game.

"Instead coaches nowadays produce clones of themselves. Cautious players with a negative attitude. It's like when you were at school. If the professor said something you accepted it at face value because he was a professor. You didn't query it.

But that doesn't mean that he was right every time.

"Imagination is your limitation. If someone tells you you can't do that you should ask 'why?' I had no coaching badges. All I'd done since I had finished kicking a football was played golf in Spain but when Newcastle came for me in 1992 we sparked something special that will never be repeated.

"That team we put together is one of the major success stories of the last 20 years. Nothing like it will ever happen again – a newly-promoted team will not threaten to win the championship because the gulf is too big now. It's all about money.

"I don't believe coaching badges are necessary. They stereotype people. All I ever did was go into things with great enthusiasm and belief and allow it to rub off on others."

Keegan, born on St. Valentine's Day in 1951, has always been a romantic. The Premier League he left in March of 2005 when quitting Manchester City, is now too mechanical, too predictable for him which is why he's turned his back on it and headed over the border, just as he walked away from so many things in the past if reality no longer matched the promises of the brochure. He was the ringmaster long before the circus came to his town and he revelled in his Geordie adventure.

"When Newcastle came calling for me it was very exciting," recalled Kevin. "John Hall phoned and said: 'Only two people can save Newcastle United and they are talking to each other right now.' That was a powerful message. We went on a roller-coaster ride, all of us together.

"Douglas Hall and Freddy Shepherd were great when I was there. John was the figurehead but they drove the club forward. And chief executive Freddie Fletcher – we called him Jockweiler – was also vital in our era.

"We mightn't have won the ultimate prize, though we should have done, but perhaps you Geordies now haven't to look so far back in history because of us. When I arrived everyone talked about Jackie Milburn and the fifties. Perhaps now it's The Entertainers."

Had Keegan beaten Alex Ferguson to the Premier League championship he would have loved it, loved it. But it was not to be, a 12-point lead miraculously achieved but not retained that pulsating season of 1995-96. However, if Sir smirked then at his victorious gallop up the rails his favourite son Eric Cantona admitted the following season, upon visiting St. James's Park, that Keegan had, indeed, a wondrous side.

Cantona had scored the lone goal that, together with Peter Schmeichel's awesome saves, won the match 1-0 at St. James's Park and led to Manchester United overhauling Newcastle for the title. A year on and Keegan's troops took savage revenge, destroying the Old Trafford aristocrats 5-0 in a match still cherished by the Toon Army.

"Oh, it was my favourite game of the lot," smiled KK. "We absolutely slaughtered them – and remember Man U were the current champions. We played them off the park. I always remember on the final whistle I went down the tunnel and was standing at the top of the stairs when the players trooped in. As he passed Cantona growled: 'You've got an effing good side' and walked on. His English was supposed to be not so good but he knew what we were about."

If the slaughter of his old tormentor Fergie was the highpoint for Keegan, I asked him if the 4-3 defeat at Liverpool during the 1995-96 run-in, when every point was a gold nugget and United had led in typical swashbuckling style, was his worst moment.

"Not really," he replied quick as a flash. "Because for all but the last few minutes we had played so well. We weren't outclassed as Man U were on the day against us. We were the better team right until near the end. Of course it killed us but for the neutral it was a pulsating spectacle. It was voted the 'Game of the Decade' in the Premiership wasn't it?"

Keegan made so many lavish signings for Newcastle in an era

when the bank was broken almost monthly in his craving for perfection that to select the greatest of the great is a monumental task capable of concentrating biased minds forever.

As we talked Keegan not unnaturally waxed lyrical over each and every one of them like a father fussing over his large brood. The club record was smashed through a succession of eye-popping deals culminating in the emotional return home for Geordie Alan Shearer at a world record £15m. However, when I pressed him for his best signing of the lot KK finally succumbed. The chosen one Peter Beardsley, so good Newcastle bought him twice.

Beardsley had partnered Keegan in black and white stripes as promotion was won in the 1980s and had made such an impression he was brought back by his old team-mate to help spark a new revolution.

"When you have a goalscorer in the team you're blessed and you're equally blessed by the presence of a creator," Keegan told me. "So when you have both in one player then you have the complete deal.

"Peter could do both equally well. He was a giver, not a taker by nature. He enjoyed making a goal for Andy Cole as much as scoring one himself. Indeed, I had to rollick him a couple of times for passing to Andy, who missed when Pedro could have scored himself. He was very special to the club, a Geordie who understood his own folk and was on the same wavelength as myself.

"But I was lucky I had so many truly wonderful players at Newcastle and I appreciate every one of them to this day. Not just the ones I bought but the home-grown lads who responded to those I put around them, players who perhaps didn't realise the standard they could attain.

"Not many people might expect me to talk about Brian Kilcline, for example, considering the big-name players who followed him but he was absolutely crucial to me at the time. He settled us down and got us going.

"Philippe Albert was immense for his finesse while Rob Lee at £700,000 was superb value for money, the signing who glued the jigsaw together. Then there was Andy Cole for his goals alongside Peter, Sir Les who followed him, David Ginola with all his Gallic flair, and of course Alan Shearer at the end of it all.

"Having said all that let's not forget the likes of Darren Peacock, who often stood on the bridge by himself because Bez and Albert loved to get forward."

Many of Kevin's deals had a touch of the offbeat, that flamboyant wackiness that was synonymous with the Keegan years. Like the time KK sat in the car park outside of a hotel in Wetherby arguing on the phone with his directors over whether or not Beardsley was too old (33, incidentally) before strolling inside to sign a genius.

Or the occasion when a message was left on the windscreen of a missing Andy Cole's car, spotted in Bristol city centre, telling him to get in touch with City urgently because Keegan was in for him. Andy, a bachelor, was actually in a nearby laundry doing his washing! And what about the hilarious exchange after a deal for Tino Asprilla was completed in Italy. Freddie Fletcher enthusiastically shook the hand of the Parma president, saying "thank you very much", to which a bemused interpreter asked: "Why did you shake hands? He's just called you a little s**t", no doubt a reference to some heavy bargaining by United.

In those merriest of days fun ran through United like words through a stick of seaside rock. Both on and off the field of battle. Perhaps Kevin's most controversial signing, however, was the £7.5m import of Asprilla, a colourful if outrageously wild superstar from Colombia who was playing in Italy's Serie A.

"A lot of Press from outside the North East needed a scapegoat when we failed to win the Premier League title and they settled on Tino," Keegan told me. "That was totally wrong, totally unfair. I honestly think that Asprilla only had two poor games for us all the time he was there. I wanted him because he was world class and all the rubbish about his wild days never bothered me a bit. Some of it was scandalous but I never wavered and I got top-class backing from the board.

"I had seen Tino play for Colombia against England at Wembley and was struck by his enthusiasm and work rate as well as his obvious ability. No, we didn't lose the Premier League because of Asprilla, but because too many people around the club, off and on the field, didn't know how to win something. Beardsley apart I don't think there was anyone else who had achieved the ultimate prize."

Apart form the Geordie Messiah himself of course, twice European Footballer of the Year, European Cup winner, a champion with Liverpool and Hamburg, England skipper and their future manager.

Nowadays he's never lured by a live match on television and knows not a thing of Scottish football despite his new power base in Glasgow.

Sure, Keegan talks regularly on the phone to cherished old players like Peter Beardsley, but that is the limit of his involvement in today's regimented game. His new life and new challenge, he tells me, is with Soccer Circus and he would eventually love to bring it to Newcastle.

The plan is that the Glasgow venture will be the first of many branches worldwide and he told me: "The Geordies would love it and I'd love to take Soccer Circus to Newcastle. I'm not saying it'll be the next place we go but it would be great to eventually make it to Tyneside."

KK calls it 'his future', adding: "This will be bigger than Manchester United. I've always been about a challenge and this is it. Football is no longer about romance but finances. The fun has gone.

"I'll never watch a game now and I don't miss it. I follow the news about my old clubs Newcastle, Man City and Fulham but that's all. If anyone questioned me in depth about what was happening generally in football I'd no doubt fail."

Kevin left his last job at Manchester City by mutual consent in March of 2005. After four years in the job and the challenge of trying to wake another sleeping giant like Newcastle, he walked away calling time on his fourth and he insists last managerial commitment.

"I just got stale," he explained. "If you don't enjoy it, if you don't look forward to working with your players, then you have to get out. It got to the stage where I thought: 'Hold on, is this what I want to do with the rest of my life?' Some people are happy to stay where they are forever but if I'm not enjoying something, I move on."

Keegan works every night until 9pm, having thrown himself enthusiastically into Soccer Circus as he's done with whatever currently takes his mind. He's hands-on, the painter of the café, the guy who bought the old turnstiles form Middlesbrough's Ayresome Park at an antique shop near Leeds and a row of wooden seats from Stoke's abandoned Victoria Ground and transported them up to Glasgow.

"Here football is still fun and anyone can play it," he explained. "The coaches only want the cream but ordinary guys love soccer and they should be able to take part. We give them that opportunity to indulge themselves."

When it eventually came time to say goodbye, to store away the most pleasant of memories for yet another day, the saviour of Newcastle United both as a player and manager smiled that infectious smile of old. "Howay the lads," he shouted and waved. It was time to head back to the circus!

PERFECT 10

The Matches

Football games stand out in the memory for a variety of reasons. Some personal, some romantic or sentimental, others because they are stepping-stones in history.

Every fan has his favourite memories. Games where heroes abound, where victory was always inevitable, where goals were never tap-ins but full blooded and arrowed straight at the heart.

I am no different. They come thick and fast...the Inter-Cities Fairs Cup final of 1969 because it's the last time United won anything of consequence and, by gosh, because I was there. The same age as the players on the field, I expected many more such glints of silverware down the years. None came and I'm still waiting, still optimistic of heart. That's what we Geordies do best – wait and be optimistic.

The 5-0 victory over champions Manchester United epitomised the Keegan fantasy years and wound be in the top 10 of any Magpie. Without a doubt. The chip of Philippe Albert. Can't you just see it in the mind's eye? Europe, of course, plays a major part in fond recollections. A 3-2 Champions League victory over mighty Barcelona. Can it get much better? Well, the last-minute winner by Craig Bellamy away to Feyenoord to clinch qualification for the second phase of the Champions League was a heart attack inducer. And a 5-0 triumph in Antwerp an arrogant swagger of superiority.

'The Match That Never Was', a 4-3 FA Cup victory over

Nottingham Forest on the way to Wembley, was unique and therefore special. Any victory over Sunderland is cherished and any large win such as 7-1 against Leicester City to round off promotion and 8-0 at home to Sheffield Wednesday in Sir Bobby Robson's first home game.

There are special matches because of special people, of course. Skipper Bob Moncur scored a hat-trick in the two-legged Inter-Cities Fairs Cup final when his job was supposed to be to deny the crack Hungarians at the back. Alan Shearer notched five times in Robson's cherished coming as a manager. And SuperMac's home debut was, well, as perfect as it gets. A hat-trick against the mightiest Liverpool side of all time and carried off on a stretcher after charging through in search of a fourth goal.

Some matches of stature haven't made my ten. For example the Premier League's official best encounter of all time involved Newcastle, but in a 4-3 seesaw defeat at Liverpool and, however exhilarating, the final outcome prevents me from including it. It wasn't perfect you see! I personally much enjoyed Newcastle's 2-0 victory over Manchester United at Old Trafford in the early seventies because it came only a week after the humiliation of losing to non-League Hereford United in the FA Cup and so wiped the smile off a million faces. Enjoyed, too, the two FA Cup semi-final victories which brought the 1990s to an end because they once again took us to the Twin Towers on chariots of hope.

Beating Inter Milan in the Bob Moncur era and Juventus when Shearer was king, both times at St. James's Park, stand out because defeating any Italian Serie A team is a stripe on the arm. I could go on and on. Anyway, may I present my Perfect 10 Matches, not necessarily in order of preference but merely as they leap from my memory bank.

The scoreboard says it all as United announce their return to European competition in emphatic style against Belgian side Royal Antwerp

179

29 May 1969
NEWCASTLE UNITED 3
UJPEST DOZSA 0

11 June 1969
UJPEST DOZSA 2
NEWCASTLE UNITED 3

I've coupled these games together because, as a two-legged European final, one is incomplete without the other.

Maybe these days Hungarian football means little but once they were giants. After Ferenc Puskas came to Wembley to destroy England and its reputation, Ujpest took up the sword at club level. The magical Magyars had beaten Fairs Cup holders Leeds United home and away in the semi-finals with Don Revie hailing them as "the best club side in Europe." Other legendary managers – Liverpool's Bill Shankly and Jock Stein of Celtic – also tipped Ujpest for the trophy. But what did they know? United crushed the hot favourites home and away and if skipper Bob Moncur was the centre stage star then the chorus was pretty impressive too.

More than an hour had gone goalless in front of an expectant full house at St. James's Park before the floodgates were opened by Moncur, smashing home after keeper Szentmihalyi had saved from Wyn Davies. Within 10 minutes Moncur, who normally got a nosebleed crossing the halfway line, had played a one-two with Benny Arentoft to strike a daisy cutter into the corner of the net. Oh, the shock of it all.

The dainty Jimmy Scott added a third, bravely lifting the ball over the advancing keeper, and on a night deep into June United arrived in Budapest in the driving seat to complete the job. Except that Ujpest, stung and bitterly hurt, rallied to prove they

European joy for manager Joe Harvey (above) and striker Wyn Davies
(below), who proudly show off the Inter-Cities Fairs Cup in 1969

were indeed more than a decent side. I was sitting next to the Clown Prince of Soccer, Len Shackleton, and by the interval with the home side two goals up on the night we were fearing the worst. Ferenc Bene (30 minutes) and Janos Gorocs (43) had scored in a tidal wave of attacks but Joe Harvey was determined that his 51st birthday would not be spoiled. "Score once and this lot will fold," he growled and wasn't he right?

Moncur – who else – volleyed home within a minute of the restart and Ujpest's balloon was burst. Arentoft (53) and sub Alan Foggon (68) scored and every Geordie heart pounded with pride as United sealed a 6-2 aggregate triumph.

Afterwards Arentoft, still in his playing kit, was standing in the corridor phoning his match report to a paper back home in Copenhagen. Can you imagine Steven Gerrard belling the *Liverpool Echo* after winning the European Cup?

Inter-Cities Fairs Cup final, 1st leg – St. James's Park

Newcastle United 3-0 Ujpest Dozsa
United goalscorers: Moncur 2, Scott
United team: McFaul, Craig, Clark, Gibb, Burton, Moncur,
Scott, B Robson, Davies, Arentoft, Sinclair (Elliott).
Attendance: 59,234

Inter-Cities Fairs Cup final, 2nd leg – Dozsa-Stadion

Ujpest Dozsa 2-3 Newcastle United
United goalscorers: Arentoft, Foggon, Moncur
United team: McFaul, Craig, Clark, Gibb, Burton, Moncur,
Scott (Foggon), B Robson, Davies, Arentoft, Sinclair.
Attendance: 34,000

United pose with the Inter-Cities Fairs Cup, following the 6-2 aggregate success of Ujpest Dozsa, 1969. Back row left to right: Ollie Burton, Tommy Gibb, Eric Ross, David Smith (trainer), David Craig, Frank Clark, Alan Foggon, Wyn Davies, Bob Moncur, Joe Harvey (manager). Front row left to right: Jackie Sinclair, Ian McFaul, Bryan Robson, Benny Arentoft, Jim Scott

20 October 1996

NEWCASTLE UNITED 5
MANCHESTER UNITED 0

Read that scoreline again, because you don't often see one like it. Manchester United were taken to bits. Schmeichel, Gary Neville, Pallister, Scholes, Beckham, Butt, Cantona et al.

If Newcastle's first goal was scrappy, a header from Darren Peacock only just creeping across the line, then the rest were top drawer. A superb turn and cross shot from David Ginola, a Les Ferdinand trademark header, Alan Shearer close-in dagger thrust and finally the cream of the crop – Philippe Albert's audacious chip from 25 yards over the top of a bemused Schmeichel. By now we were all in seventh heaven.

The quality of the opposition made it even better – and to underline their class Manchester United went on to retain their Premiership crown.

But that day United had pinged the ball around the turf to do to Fergie's side what they normally dished out to others.

Premier League – St. James's Park

Newcastle United 5-0 Manchester United
United goalscorers: Peacock, Ginola, Ferdinand, Shearer, Albert
United team: Srnicek, Watson (Barton), Beresford, Albert,
Peacock, Lee (Clark), Batty, Beardsley, Ginola, Shearer,
Ferdinand.
Attendance: 36,579

Darren Peacock (second left), Phillipe Albert and Les Ferdinand celebrate as the
former's header gives Newcastle the lead against champions Manchester United

Phillipe Albert (left) prepares to be mobbed by team-mates after sealing a memorable
5-0 demolition of the Red Devils with a glorious chip over Peter Schmeichel

17 September 1997

NEWCASTLE UNITED 3
FC BARCELONA 2

United ace Peter Beardsley loved Tino Asprilla, insisting they were players on the same wavelength. Presumably on the field, Peter, because off it Tino was from another planet! Anyway, this was the Columbian's finest hour on Geordie patrol. He floored mighty Barca with a hat-trick and somersaulted his way into Geordie folklore.

Barcelona were top drawer in those days as well as now and United had to confront them on European Champions League duty without the injured Alan Shearer. No matter, Newcastle roared into a 3-0 lead to put down a marker for every other top continental club to take warning.

If Asprilla ran the show it was Keith Gillespie who was the inspirational provider on a glorious night. United's first was a penalty after Tino himself had been felled but his second and third owed much to the blinding pace of Gillespie skinning full-back Sergi. On each occasion Asprilla soared like a bird on the wing to blast headers past keeper Hesp.

The immense physical effort United had put in told late on and Barca surged back with late goals from Luis Enrique and Luis Figo. We were dying for the final whistle because victory was so deserved and when it came emotion poured down the terraces.

European Champions League Group C – St. James's Park

Newcastle United 3-2 FC Barcelona
United goalscorer: Asprilla 3 (1 pen)
United team: Given, Barton, Beresford, Albert, Watson,
Gillespie, Batty, Lee, Barnes (Ketsbaia), Tomasson (Peacock),
Asprilla.
Attendance: 35,274

Barcelona goalkeeper Ruud Hesp can only look back in despair
as Faustino Asprilla celebrates one of his three goals

13 November 2002

FEYENOORD 2
NEWCASTLE UNITED 3

On an autumn evening in Rotterdam's De Kuip Stadium the Magpies created a little piece of history and thousands of Geordie hearts stopped beating for a split second.

United became the first club in the Champions League to qualify for the second group stage after losing the opening three games. Some recovery that, and it was achieved with an injury-time goal.

Newcastle stormed into a two-goal lead against their first-ever Euro opponents back in 1968 with Alan Shearer and Craig Bellamy confusing the Feyenoord defence and Kieron Dyer's rapid support runs causing havoc.

Shearer set up Bellamy for the first with a cushioned header which saw the Welshman streaking away to beat the keeper from a wide position. Within four minutes of the break Hugo Viana had scored a stunning second. One-paced but with a good left foot, Viana never made it at St. James's Park but this was a glimpse of a talent undoubtedly there beneath the surface. The Portuguese midfielder took a Dyer pass to unleash an unstoppable shot from the edge of the box.

Against the run of play Feyenoord sub Bombarda pulled a goal back and as the home crowd at last came to life Luring scored an equaliser.

Geordie hopes had died in their throats but deep into injury time United broke away and Dyer looked to have missed a golden opportunity, shooting straight at the Dutch keeper Lodewijks. Oh, the despair. However, the ball rebounded into no-man's land for Bellamy to jump onto it and screw the ball into the net from an acute angle. What a way to finish a special night.

European Champions League First Stage Group E
– De Kuip Stadium

Feyenoord 2-3 Newcastle United
United goalscorers: Bellamy 2, Viana
United team: Given, Hughes, Griffin, O'Brien, Dabizas, Dyer, Jenas, Speed, Viana (Bernard), Bellamy, Shearer.
Attendance: 45,000

Manager Bobby Robson remains pensive as the United bench celebrate Craig Bellamy's dramatic late winning goal against Feyenoord in Rotterdam

21 August 1971

NEWCASTLE UNITED 3
LIVERPOOL 2

This was the day SuperMac said hello to Tyneside and we all fell in love with a brash kid who had pace like fire and a shot like a cannonball.

Macdonald had been quiet in his opening two games in London against Crystal Palace and Spurs and with an all-conquering Liverpool side due at St. James's Park next we had no reason to expect fireworks. At least we thought that because we hadn't yet been introduced to SuperMac! He was man-marked by the *Anfield Iron*, Tommy Smith, who was his own health warning. He used to tell you what he was going to do to you! Emlyn Hughes got Liverpool off to the expected start with a penalty but then David Young, never more than a journeyman, was hacked down by Kevin Keegan of all people in the away 18-yard box and the first of Macdonald's goals ripped the back of the net from the spot.

However, the goal which heralded SuperMac's arrival came just before the interval. Tommy Gibb played a ball into Malcolm's feet, he knocked it outside Tommy Smith and accelerated past him to smack a left-foot shot straight as an arrow into the top far corner. The 'whoosh' could be heard right around the ground, followed by a great roar of admiration which could have wakened the dead. In that split second a love affair was born.

Midway through the second half came the hat-trick. Terry Hibbitt clipped a deft pass inside to John Tudor, who touched it on to SuperMac coming in on the diagonal. He took a touch with his left foot to make half-a-yard of space and whipped a shot past Ray Clemence. Three ruddy one! Liverpool were petrified of the 21-year-old upstart by now and when he galloped through again like a tank on the charge Clemence met him head on, six studs unintentionally in the face, and it was stretcher time.

The next thing Macdonald knew was waking up in the dressing room and Frank Clark telling him Newcastle had won 3-2. Liverpool had pulled a goal back late on (through a certain KK) but not a solitary soul cared. A new superstar was born.

First Division – St. James's Park

Newcastle United 3-2 Liverpool
United goalscorer: Macdonald 3 (1 pen)
United team: McFaul, Craig, Clark, Gibb, Burton, Moncur,
Dyson, Tudor, Macdonald, Young, Hibbitt.
Attendance: 39,720

Supermac, in pre-season pose, made a huge impact on his St. James's Park bow

9 March 1974

NEWCASTLE UNITED 4
NOTTINGHAM FOREST 3

Everything happened in a momentous run to the FA Cup final at Wembley but nothing quite like this! Controversy walked hand in hand with United in this sixth-round tie. Forest were struggling to keep in touch with the Second Division pacesetters but found themselves cruising at 3-1 against 10 men.

Bowyer put the visitors ahead early doors only for David Craig to equalise but instead of the great home surge O'Kane lashed a 20-yarder and Lyall scored from the penalty spot. To make a bad job shocking Pat Howard was sent off for disputing the spot-kick.

Frustration engulfed a stadium full with 54,500 spectators. Enraged at the penalty decision and the sending off of Howard United fans poured onto the pitch after an hour and referee Gordon Kew hurriedly led the teams to the sanctity of the dressing rooms where they stayed for eight minutes.

Humiliation as well as defeat apparently awaited us all except that on the resumption Terry McDermott notched a penalty himself, John Tudor crashed in a diving header for the equaliser and Bob Moncur – him again – volleyed home the apparent winner. However, all was not as it seemed. Forest appealed to the FA that the crowd disturbance had adversely affected them and a replay was ordered at a neutral Goodison Park. It ended 0-0 and a few days later two exhausted teams did it all again at the same venue. This time Malcolm Macdonald, who surprisingly hadn't scored in the four-goal deluge, got the all-important winner through pace and aggression, two of his most vital commodities.

FA Cup 6th round – St. James's Park

Newcastle United 4-3 Nottingham Forest
United goalscorers: Craig, McDermott (pen), Tudor, Moncur
United team: McFaul, Craig (Kennedy), Clark, McDermott, Howard, Moncur, Barrowclough, Smith, Macdonald, Tudor, Hibbitt.
Attendance: 54,500

John Tudor's diving header brings 10-man Newcastle level against Nottingham Forest in the 1974 FA Cup quarter-final at St. James's Park

13 September 1994

ROYAL ANTWERP 0
NEWCASTLE UNITED 5

This was United's first match back in Europe and didn't they make it extra special! Rob Lee led the parade, scoring a hat-trick of headers. Yes, headers which were hardly Rob's style. Scott Sellars and Steve Watson completed the victory parade.

It was an avalanche. United were one-up after only 50 seconds, two-up in eight minutes and three-up by half-time. That's taking Europe by the scruff of the neck. Antwerp weren't a bad side, it was merely that United were irrepressible.

"We showed that you can go into Europe and play exciting, attacking football and not travel in fear," declared Kevin Keegan, the master of the full frontal approach. "Not only did we make people sit up and take notice in Belgium but we won through by scoring 10 goals and swamping Antwerp 5-2 in the return leg at St. James's Park. Even great teams of the past would have been proud of such a demolition job."

UEFA Cup 1st round, 1st leg – Bosuilstadion

Royal Antwerp 0-5 Newcastle United
United goalscorers: Lee 3, Sellars, Watson
United team: Srnicek, Hottiger, Beresford, Albert, Peacock, Fox, Venison, Lee, Sellars, Beardsley (Watson), Cole (Jeffrey).
Attendance: 19,700

A travelling United fan shows his gratitude to manager Kevin Keegan
following the impressive 5-0 mauling of Royal Antwerp

9 May 1993

NEWCASTLE UNITED 7
LEICESTER CITY 1

United were crowned Football League champions in an orgy of goals to have chairman Sir John Hall literally singing their praises. Normally a nervous spectator, Hall got so carried away when Newcastle were six-up at half-time that he wandered from private box to private box with a bottle in his hand pouring everyone a drink. He even climbed up to the television gantry to sing a song to the crew!

"No one could have lived with us," gushed Kevin Keegan. "As a one-off game it was as perfect as I could have wished – 7-1 is some way to round off a championship season isn't it? With a couple of minutes to go to half-time I stood with Terry McDermott looking round the ground. We were six goals ahead and the whole place was a sea of black and white. You couldn't hear yourself speak for the din."

David Kelly grabbed a hat-trick on what was to be his last appearance for the club. Andy Cole matched it, and Rob Lee notched a gem of a goal.

A fabulous, fabulous day had started with local pop group *Lindisfarne* playing on the pitch and clowns dancing. It ended with United amassing 96 points and 29 victories to lift two championship trophies. Nice one, eh?

First Division – St. James's Park

Newcastle United 7-1 Leicester City
United goalscorers: Kelly 3, Cole 3, Lee
United team: Srnicek, Venison, Beresford (Peacock), Scott,
Howey (Kilcline), Lee, Robinson, Clark, Sellars, Cole, Kelly.
Attendance: 30,129

Sir John Hall cannot contain his delight after seeing KK's First
Division champions demolish Leicester City at St. James's

19 September 1999

NEWCASTLE UNITED 8
SHEFFIELD WEDNESDAY 0

It was a great day for one Pressman – me! Not so good for Kevin Pressman, the Aunt Sally in goal for Wednesday. He was hit for eight goals and United's bomber-in-chief Alan Shearer notched five of them.

Both clubs were caught up in a relegation dogfight to stay in the Premier League but while this victory signalled the start of a marvellous recovery by the Mags, opponents Wednesday tumbled into Football League obscurity.

Aaron Hughes began the demolition after 10 minutes, heading home Kieron Dyer's cross then Shearer took control with a hat-trick – a deft flick from Nobby Solano's pass, a characteristic power penalty, then getting in front of Des Walker to meet Dyer's centre. Dyer was running the Owls ragged and he scored himself after the interval to make it 5-0 from a blocked shot by Gary Speed.

The Welshman then knocked in a header and Shearer wrapped it all up with a half volley and another penalty. The Robson revolution was underway.

Premier League – St. James's Park

Newcastle United 8-0 Sheffield Wednesday
United goalscorers: Hughes, Shearer 5 (1 pen), Dyer, Speed
United team: Harper, Barton, Hughes, Goma, Domi, Solano
(Glass), Lee, Speed, Dyer (Robinson), Ketsbaia (McClen),
Shearer.
Attendance: 36,619

A dream start for Bobby Robson (above, saluting the fans at the end of the 1999-
2000 season) as Sheffield Wednesday are hit for eight in his first game in charge

18 October 1992

SUNDERLAND 1
NEWCASTLE UNITED 2

I could have taken any Newcastle victory over their arch rivals as a warming memory but selected this one for a couple of reasons. It was on their patch, which made it even more satisfying and completed the most startling of beginnings to a new season.

The match was a contest between Sunderland's determination and the finesse of Keegan's cavaliers. An own goal broke the deadlock in the 12th minute. Barry Venison attacked down the right, Gavin Peacock flicked on to Rob Lee who pulled a low cross into the middle where Gary Owers, under pressure from Kevin Brock, slid the ball into his own net from close range.

United's crisp inter-passing play marked them out as the classier side but the battling Wearsiders shocked them with an equaliser out of the blue 21 minutes from time. An Owers right-wing corner fell to the feet of Newcastle-born Gordon Armstrong who had only been on the pitch for four minutes as a sub. He rifled home a low shot from eight yards.

United had gone to Roker Park with 10 successive victories behind them. Were the old enemy of all people going to be the ones to stop them dead in their tracks? Of course not. In the 76th minute Brian Atkinson conceded a free-kick 20 yards out from the Roker End where the Newcastle fans were massed. I was sitting smack bang in line with the ball and when Liam

O'Brien struck it I could follow the swerve as it cleared the defensive wall and left the keeper for dead. It was an awesome strike, typical of the big Irishman on dead balls.

This was United's first win at Roker Park for 36 years, it meant they had won 11 matches out of 11 to start the season, and were already 10 points clear at the top of the table en route to the First Division title and promotion.

First Division – Roker Park

Sunderland 1-2 Newcastle United
United goalscorers: Owers (own goal), O'Brien
United team: Wright, Venison (Kilcline), Beresford, Howey,
Scott, Lee, Brock (Bracewell), O'Brien, Clark, Peacock, Kelly.
Attendance: 30,088

David Kelly is denied by a sliding challenge in the dramatic 2-1 victory over Sunderland at Roker Park – Newcastle's first win there in 36 years

PERFECT 10

ALSO AVAILABLE IN THE SERIES